SPRINGFIELD RESURGENT

HOW A PROUD CITY BUILT A FISCALLY SUSTAINABLE FUTURE

BY TIMOTHY J. PLANTE

Introduction by Mayor Domenic J. Sarno

First printed June 2021

The paper used in this book meets the minimum requirements of the
American National Standard for Information Services
ANSI Z39.48-1984 (Permanence of Paper for Printed Library Materials).

Cover designed by UKG Inc.
Interior design by Diana Davis, Upright Arts, Inc.

ISBN 9780972330077 (print version)
ISBN 9780972330091 (e-version)
Printed and bound in the United States of America.

UKG Inc.
900 Chelmsford Street
Lowell, MA 01851
Phone: +1 800-225-1561

TABLE OF CONTENTS

Timothy J. Plante

M any of the initiatives described in these pages came to light well before our country experienced the impact of COVID-19. Others, however, were unceremoniously and indefinitely paused when the pandemic reached our city and redirected Springfield's full attention and resources to supporting essential services and public safety. Be reminded as you read this book that the lessons learned hold true, even though some of the gains may have been temporarily lost.

John Butler, Chief Financial Officer, UKG

L ike many working cities across America, Springfield, Massachusetts, has faced a decades-long uphill battle to rebuild its economy and civic infrastructure. While the decline of the manufacturing sector left many urban centers in a lurch, budgetary constraints in Springfield compounded by the effects of a tough economic and political climate have continued to build extreme barriers to the city's recovery.

In any environment or context, the task of revitalizing a city can seem impossibly daunting. Yet, for Springfield, building better processes internally and gaining oversight of the city's labor data opened the door for opportunity and millions of dollars to be reinvested back into the community.

UKG (Ultimate Kronos Group) is a partner to thousands of U.S. government agencies across all 50 states, each focused on balancing the needs of constituents while advancing processes in the era of digital transformation. The UKG suite of HCM, payroll, HR service delivery, and workforce management solutions helps cities bring processes into the future to control their labor costs, minimize compliance risk, and maintain accuracy. We have seen it all, from working with change agents bringing tangible improvements to some of the nation's most economically depressed urban centers to supporting the forward-thinking visionaries building the smart cities of the future.

In all our experience with customers, it is rare to see a city turn around to the extent that Springfield has. From establishing good data governance to investing in system-level changes and data analytics that have given the city strategic labor insights, Springfield proves that those who are ready to embrace digital transformation and willing to overhaul internal processes will prosper.

Though, to be candid, not every administration wants to look closely at their labor data. As the saying goes, "Don't ask the question if you're not prepared to hear the answer." But officials in Springfield, undeterred, leapt at the opportunity to modernize their systems and peel back the precarious layers of their finances and labor data to unearth a series of underlying issues that, ready or not, they needed to address. Springfield's leaders fixed the city from the inside out, freeing up resources, funding, and people power to drive a remarkably ambitious city-wide turnaround.

It's for this reason that UKG urged officials in Springfield to tell their story. The city overcame extreme adversity to foster fiscal sustainability. Collaborative leadership and systematic checks and balances formed the basis for achieving what many would have otherwise deemed an impossible financial turnaround.

Springfield's proverbial "road to revival" is a guidepost for state and local leaders. It implores America's cities and metro areas to follow the money, get to the root cause, and put in place digital systems and data-based policies that can correct and prevent future financial neglect. As Springfield Mayor Domenic J. Sarno would attest, you can't do it all, and you especially can't do it all *well* until you get your finances in order and hold your workforce accountable to play by the rules.

At a fundamental level, UKG believes that great organizations are powered by great people, and the people of Springfield did something together that every city in America can learn from.

INTRODUCTION

Mayor Domenic J. Sarno, City of Springfield

Eleven years ago, in 2009, when Springfield, Massachusetts regained home rule after a challenging few years under the auspices of the state-run Finance Control Board, most observers quite simply figured our city would fall off the face of the earth. Given the events of the preceding years, it was hard to argue with those observers. Happily, however, that didn't happen.

Instead, Springfield rebounded from its dark days and has moved to a brighter, more prosperous future. We stabilized the city's finances, turning a $41 million deficit in 2004 into a $50 million surplus in 2020. After flirting with near-junk-bond status, our credit rating is now the best in the city's history. We leveraged this financial strength to generate $4.7 billion in economic development, increase public safety, and make substantial improvements to our public schools.

After a long period of doubt, Springfield and its citizens have confidence in what the city can do on their behalf. That confidence hasn't been gained through smoke and mirrors—we earned it by building, rebuilding, creating jobs, creating a community. This is our renaissance. But without the right financial foundation, none of this would be possible.

Residents and businesses alike want to see financial stability and strength. They want to see clean, solid financials. They have every right to hold their local leaders accountable, so that when the hard times come—when an EF-3 tornado cuts through your city or a global pandemic forces an economic shutdown— together we are prepared to take the punch and keep moving forward.

Through a combination of "financial tough love" and hard choices, a strong and dedicated team, and the implementation of the right financial and labor management software, the right analytics, and the right processes (complete with checks and balances), we finally got our financial house in order. Everything we have accomplished in Springfield—the marquee achievements as well as the small yet meaningful projects that have bettered our communities—relied on this.

In the pages that follow, my chief administrative and financial officer (CAFO) Timothy J. Plante—a.k.a. TJ—describes how Springfield has overcome tremendous fiscal challenges while outlining the work that's needed to continue our forward momentum. It's a perspective only he can share, though TJ would be first to ascribe Springfield's progress to the work, experience, and compassion of many—from City Hall to the State House, and from our neighborhoods to our business district. This story doesn't belong to any individual. It belongs to all of us.

CHAPTER ONE

A Financial Reckoning

The words may be harsh, but they are the unfortunate reality. In 2004, in countless ways, large and small, Springfield was simply a broken city.

From almost any perspective, the third largest city in the Commonwealth of Massachusetts was haunted by failure: school performance, crime, economic decline, underfunded pensions, and underwhelming housing values. Back in the early '80s, budgets were cut across the city following the passage of Proposition 2½, a Massachusetts law that limits property taxes and the ability to support core city services. By the early-to-mid '90s, our police force headcount had reduced dramatically—we were down 400 police officers—and the results were hardly surprising. The City-Data.com crime index for Springfield shows that violent crime on city streets in 2004 was nearly four times the national average. Businesses responded by decamping for nearby locations, hollowing out the downtown districts and leaving gaping economic holes throughout the city.

Springfield had lost control of its bottom line. It was the appalling state of the city's finances that created the shrieking alarm that reached all the way to the governor's office at the State House in Boston. For a variety of reasons—too many reasons, in fact—a city with a $442 million budget simply wasn't living within its means. After years of politicians kicking the can down the road, the tab was now long overdue. When it was all tallied up, Springfield, the largest city on the Connecticut River and the unofficial capital of Western Massachusetts, found itself flat on its back and staring down a shocking $41 million deficit—and few prospects to get off the mat and regain its footing.

For years, the city based its budget on 100% of its real estate and personal property revenue but managed to collect only 92% of that figure. It was an inherently unsustainable financial model that, over the course of a few years, led to the city's financial day of reckoning. Worse, the city government "didn't know what it didn't know" because there were no central systems, no checks and balances. Virtually every important financial and operational record was based on manual processes and homegrown systems. The impact on property tax collections—a crucial source of income in a city of roughly 153,000 residents—translated into millions of dollars in unclaimed income. At one point, there were $2.5 million in back taxes owed by bar owners stretching back six or seven years. One owner owed $700,000. The few computer systems in place didn't integrate, and internal controls were completely lacking, helping these scofflaws evade detection.

As a result, Springfield developed a severe cash flow problem that, at times, made it very difficult to pay vendors in a timely fashion. The first obligation, of course, was to meet weekly employee payroll—and that often meant juggling (and postponing) vendor payments, sometimes for months, while awaiting the arrival of quarterly aid monies from the state. A vendor might perform work in October but not get paid until January. The check—printed, signed, and ready to go—would sit in a vault until we had the cash in our bank accounts to ensure it didn't bounce. It was not an enviable situation, to say the least.

★ ★ ★

The City of Springfield became my home in 2007. I was hired as the municipal budget director and thereafter held positions as chief financial officer for both the city and the School Department before assuming my current responsibilities as Springfield's chief administrative and financial officer (CAFO). My ally and friend, Pat Roach—now the chief financial and operations officer for Springfield Public Schools—started working for the city around the same time. Thinking back on the things we witnessed in those early days, it was like being a new sheriff and walking into a lawless Wild West town.

Pat was hired as a financial accountant in the city auditor's office in 2005. On his very first day on the job, he walked across the street to the Department of Elder Affairs, which had requested some bookkeeping assistance. Simple enough, Pat thought—until he got there.

"I met this nice man who proceeded to open a large drawer that was packed with dozens of envelopes containing cash," Pat recalled. "On each one, there was a handwritten number. I couldn't believe my eyes. In the safe, they stored stacks of checks—all signed, but with no payee written on them. 'You can't deposit the cash in a city account,' he helpfully explained. 'You'll never get it back.'

"So, whenever they needed some funds—you know, to rent a bus for a seniors' day trip or something—they'd dip into their cash drawer or fill in a payee on one of the blank checks. They even had a shadow bank account for Elder Affairs. Now, I'd stress that I don't think this was some scam they were running for their personal benefit. It was just how business was done. It was a wild first day."

We later found that it wasn't any better in the School Department. With a $300 million budget, school finances were being managed by a single controller who couldn't possibly keep up with the challenges. (By contrast, a $30 million portion of school grant funds was managed by five accountants.) Archaic systems prevented us from seeing the waste, fraud, abuse, and other unfortunate lapses that, beneath the surface, were so prevalent.

Student activity accounts—ones that collect cash from fundraising activities or a vocational program that might bring in money when students work on automotive repairs, for example—had zero internal controls. Money for a carpentry project paid for materials that somehow ended up... in Rhode Island. A school store cash register became a slush fund. One teacher even started selling hot dogs in the classroom for cash. And we learned about a school janitor who liked to deliberately leave a door ajar each Friday night, using a pipe as a doorstop. When the automatically armed alarm would sound later that night, he would return to work, remove the pipe he placed there hours earlier, and subsequently collect the minimum of two hours of overtime pay.

* * *

By law, a city cannot operate at a deficit, which is an extraordinary event, so Springfield essentially papered over its structural deficits. While the city prepared and submitted balanced budgets to the state, in reality it had negative account balances. There's no nice way to explain this away: This was extraordinary malfeasance for a city of our size.

When the smoke cleared—that is, when a full accounting reconciliation was completed, leading to the final $41 million deficit (and near bankruptcy for the city)—the Massachusetts state government led by Gov. Mitt Romney moved in. In 2004, the state created the five-member Springfield Finance Control Board in return for a $52 million no-interest loan to cover the city's shortfall.

Initially headed by Massachusetts Revenue Commissioner Alan LeBovidge, the Finance Control Board made it clear that it would no longer be business as usual on the Connecticut River, as it exercised near-absolute power over all financial and personnel matters—including labor contracts (payroll accounted for 70% of the city's $442 million budget). Over the following years, the Finance Control Board helped to spearhead initiatives that got to some of the root causes of the city's many problems.

But to be effective, we needed *systems* to collect, store, track, and analyze city data, and we had none. Everything—revenue, expenses, reconciliations—was handled through paper-driven processes and paper-reliant systems. Unsurprisingly, nothing happened in real time. Procurement and payables featured multiple routings, and approvals could literally take weeks. Adjustments required months. Our people were making day-to-day decisions using months-old data. From an analytics perspective, there was zero visibility.

The only positive aspect of our formerly manual processes and terrible chart of accounts was that it gave the finance team tremendous motivation to make lots of changes, if only to escape the painful red tape that was in place. When Springfield Mayor Domenic J. Sarno was elected to his first term in 2007, he led his administration to embrace data as a change agent—a tool to promote change, not just a means to measure it.

Mayor Sarno—the city's longest-serving mayor following his reelection in 2019—had previously served as city council president and a member of the Springfield Finance Control Board, under whose guidance the city selected a financial management software program called Munis. Munis integrates all of the core accounting functions you need to operate a city government: general ledger, payroll, accounts payable, accounts receivable, contract management, asset tracking, and more. This software was our big opportunity to put in place the internal controls we desperately needed and to streamline processes so we could effectively support a broad set of cost-cutting initiatives.

For more than a year, we had a team working offsite full time to interview people from every department and build process maps showing the steps needed to complete basic tasks. The goal was to use the Munis system to streamline and automate those tasks and make the city's finance department much more efficient. Though it wasn't too surprising that we soon uncovered a hair-curling set of processes that redefined how badly red tape can hamper an organization.

Within the Office of Procurement we found perhaps the best example—or worst example, if you ask me—of how far Springfield had lost its way. We created a simple scenario: One of our school principals needs to order some pencils for her classrooms. We found that our purchase process required more than 30 separate steps and could take as long as six months to complete. Purchases required 18 different approvals—and there were no thresholds. And remember, this was a paper-based process: Someone entered data on a computer, only to print it out and give the paper—through interoffice mail—to the next stakeholder. It was like this across the city. Every school used paper forms, and every school clerk had… a typewriter. (To be candid, many of the employees, especially those with long tenures, didn't really want or appreciate change. Typewriters were just fine by them.) Every process wasted time and money, with little accountability or control. It was a recipe for failure.

Then, in July 2007, our Munis implementation went live, and the data started to trickle in. That's when life started to get better for the finance department in Springfield. Now we had actionable data to help us proactively manage the city. We could inquire about a purchase, intervene on nonstandard procurements, and redirect budget dollars in time to take corrective actions. We could aggregate purchases, determine economic order quantities, negotiate volume discounts from suppliers. For major enterprises, these are hardly earth-shattering improvements, but for our city this was nothing short of revolutionary. We now had a system of record for property taxes. Thanks to our ability to see the data, back taxes started to roll in as we pursued and collected on liens. We were finally able to see the vacancies, the savings, the surpluses. For example, if the Police Department had vacancies that represented millions of dollars, the city now had visibility and the discretion to sweep that unused money, bringing it back to Springfield's centralized free cash to determine its best use—whether that be to reinvest it into overtime, vehicles, or other pressing needs. This was a powerful tool we had during the time of the Finance Control Board and remains part of our legislation today.

Within that first year we generated more than $30 million in free cash. Soon, we were sitting on $50 million in the bank, which we accumulated simply because we had the data and could control our spending.

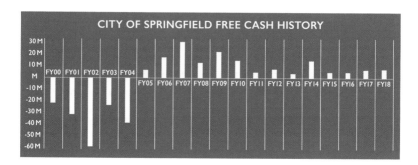

As the years went on, we uncovered more and more under-used or unused funds, which we simply attributed to poor accounting. In 2010, our schools were needlessly slashing middle-school sports and other popular programs in the name of cost cutting, when in fact they were sitting on piles of money that they didn't even know existed. Bringing back those popular programs that students and families wanted provided a boost in morale for our community. In another instance, we found three departments budgeted for professional development, yet no one was using the $250,000 that was allocated for that purpose.

During reconciliations, we identified $18.6 million in carryovers—essentially surplus funds that have since been leveraged strategically within the School Department to curb future-year problems: $4.9 million was designated for technology; $2.9 million for classroom upgrades, teacher training, and instructional materials; $2.7 went to supporting tutoring services and hiring academic intervention teachers; and the remaining balance went toward reading programs, library upgrades, and school safety and security upgrades. We later discovered an *additional* $5.4 million of unmonitored special revenue funds sitting in the school budget. The city swept it, and Pat and I were then able to collaborate on the back end to determine the best use for reinvesting that money back in the schools. It was a partnership like no other: A combination of teamwork and trust allowed us to work strategically to benefit Springfield Schools in a very immediate and impactful way.

But our work wasn't done. Next, we needed the ability to see, understand, and control labor costs—which in the mid-to-late 2000s accounted for approximately 68% (including benefits and pension) of what was then a $486.5 million annual city budget. At the time, employees were using paper timesheets to log their hours, and that data was entered into spreadsheets. We had only the faintest ability to analyze that data or detect actual trends. Further, every department had its own payroll person *and* its own union rules. Similar contracts—some of which stretched back 25–30 years—could be interpreted very differently by the various departments. In additon, there were some seriously odd terms and conditions in these labor agreements that spanned 24 separate bargaining units. Perhaps my favorite was the requirement that we give our skilled tradesmen (e.g., carpenters, plumbers, and electricians) a mandatory "shopping day" in December for them to make *personal* holiday purchases. We were literally paying for them to take a day off for Christmas shopping—an extravagant expense for a city in our financial condition.

In 2009, at the urging of the Finance Control Board and the Mayor, the city deployed an automated workforce management system from UKG (formerly Kronos Incorporated[1]), which shed light on a lot of murky areas. We used the labor data to identify waste, fraud, and abuse and to negotiate for important changes in labor contracts. It was apparent that having this technology would grant us incredible opportunity for citywide improvements.

Previously, we had no controls and no visibility, with predictably disastrous outcomes. A 30-year city employee had a near-perfect attendance record that would have made her our city's version of legendary baseball player Cal Ripken Jr., who famously played in 2,632 games without a day off. Let's just say, some of us found her record extremely hard to believe. And in our schools, before integrating our substitute management system with payroll, we had countless instances of teachers requesting a substitute to fill in for their classes without a corresponding use of paid time off. Hundreds of hours of sick time—more than $800,000 of labor expenses in a single year—were going uncharged. We experienced similar issues with timecard fraud among school staffers: Some employees

[1] Kronos Incorporated merged with Ultimate Software in 2020, becoming UKG (Ultimate Kronos Group).

would punch into their shift at a school near their home and then commute to the school where they *actually* worked.

Once the UKG system was in place and we began capturing labor data, we were finally able to close many of these gaps across the city and in our schools. The Fire Department lowered its use of overtime by 11%. Employees began to burn through sick time at appropriate rates. We reduced sick days for school employees and bargaining units while creating an incentive for good attendance. The budget for substitute teachers quickly decreased by more than $1 million, just as teacher and paraprofessional attendance rates improved. And data captured by the UKG system allowed us to easily identify and immediately correct many instances of timecard fraud. In doing so, we finally regained control of our finances.

★ ★ ★

After five years overseeing the city's financial functions, the Springfield Finance Control Board returned control to our local leaders in the summer of 2009. Once returned to home rule, the city paid back the entire multimillion state loan ahead of schedule (minus $5.2 million in city expenditures and an $8.7 million spend-down trust allocated to the Springfield Promise Program—this particular allotment was negotiated by Springfield directly with the state and the governor's office to fund scholarships for graduating seniors in our schools.) Undeniably, our ability to implement automated systems like Munis and UKG—systems that brought data and trends to the surface—was a true catalyst for Springfield's financial turnaround. The blinders were finally off. We could see our best days were ahead.

From Adversity to Advantage

June 1, 2011, was the kind of hot, muggy day we usually don't see until the dog days of August. And after a long winter, it was a promising taste of summer months ahead. Coats and hats were packed away. Sleeves were rolled up. And lunchtime crowds were enjoying a blanket of warmth—even if it was on the humid side. But over the course of the afternoon, the promise of that seasonal weather betrayed us, spawning a regionwide disaster.

At about 4:15 p.m., following a warning from the National Weather Service, an EF-3 tornado with winds topping 160 mph touched down in Westfield, Massachusetts, only a few miles from Springfield. From there, it went straight through West Springfield before it crossed the Connecticut River at 4:38 p.m. into the urban density of New England's fourth largest city—just as rush hour was getting underway.

Over the course of the next several minutes, our city experienced the worst natural disaster in its history. It wasn't unprecedented—the Worcester tornado of 1953 in central Massachusetts still ranks as the state's most devastating storm on record. But it was certainly unexpected. The tornado cut a swath of destruction 6.2 miles long and a half-mile wide that touched seven of our neighborhoods and affected about 40% of our citizens. While none of the three fatalities that day were in Springfield, more than 500 buildings were destroyed—including more than a dozen government and school facilities. We saw damage in 12 of our parks and lost some of our 200-year-old heritage trees in Court Square. From East Forest Park to Springfield College to the Sixteen Acres neighborhood, roofs were torn from buildings and homes, trees were uprooted, streetlights and wrought-iron fences were bent into pretzels, street signs flew like frisbees, and brick facades tumbled. Tens of thousands of our citizens lost power, dozens of people were sent to hospitals, and hundreds of families suddenly found themselves homeless.

* * *

In managing one of New England's largest cities, our administrative and operations teams take pride in their commitment to preparation and their ability to be ready for any situation. When the snow flies, crews in the Department of Public Works are ready to roll to keep the streets clear. When fires erupt, our firefighters answer the call. When car accidents, medical crises, power failures, and public safety incidents arise, our residents know that a strong city government is prepared to respond. But an EF-3 tornado? This was something altogether different. There's no manual for managing a tornado's aftermath, so even in the chaotic moments following the storm, as we all emerged from our basements, made urgent calls to colleagues, and made our way to the Emergency Operations Center, it was clear that our entire city faced an enormous challenge.

In the first of countless phone calls, Mayor Sarno was quickly asking his cabinet for the key stats as search and rescue operations got underway. "What's that Doobie Brothers song?" he asked. "We gotta be 'Takin' It to the Streets.'" With him leading the charge, that's exactly what we did. We walked down Main Street to survey the damage with our own eyes. We commandeered the MassMutual Center, the city's 8,000-seat arena, to use as a shelter for hundreds of displaced residents. In addition, Massachusetts Gov. Deval Patrick declared a state of emergency, activating more than 1,000 National Guard troops to help us in our rescue and recovery efforts and help maintain civic order. By 11 p.m., not even seven hours after the tornado struck, Mayor Sarno was ready to hold our first press conference to communicate what had happened and what we were going to do. More importantly, the Mayor used that platform to communicate what our shaken city needed more than ever at that hour: hope.

Springfield's entire team of first responders distinguished themselves on June 1, 2011—and for many weeks thereafter. Their responsive efforts were truly heroic. Today, Cheryl C. Clapprood is the city's police commissioner, but in 2011 she was a captain on the force. Recounting that day and the two weeks that followed, Commissioner Clapprood says that she and many others self-deployed: they worked out of a command post, set up looting details, patrolled streets, and helped people find shelter. Although brought together under poor circumstances, this was a time of bonding for Springfield Police and many in the community. All across the city, department heads had never been closer. In its earlier efforts to bring Springfield onto solid financial footing, the Finance Control Board had created "silos" among various departments and agencies. However, as Mayor Sarno described it, the tornado brought down more than roofs and buildings—it broke down the silos and barriers in our city government and allowed our shared commitment to the city to shine through. We worked collaboratively—what other choice was there, really?

★ ★ ★

By the time the sun started to rise on June 2, our top priority had been achieved: Our citizens were safe. Many were sheltered in the MassMutual Center, where they would remain for 48 hours before operations moved on a longer-term basis to Central High School. They were fed by a team deployed by our school food service partner, Sodexo. The city and the region swung into action: volunteers from the American Red Cross, Massachusetts Voluntary Organizations Active in Disasters, The Salvation Army, and hundreds more with chainsaws and rakes, meals, and blankets jumped in with a can-do attitude. Neighbors helped neighbors clear brush and debris. Blue tarpaulins spread across so many roofs became the unofficial city flag.

While this volunteer spirit was a backbone of our recovery efforts, it was equally clear to us that we were looking at an extraordinary unplanned cost. In the preceding three years, on the heels of the Great Recession, Springfield's property values had plummeted by more than $1 billion. Destruction from the tornado contributed an additional loss of more than $428 million. Unemployment rates had recently touched 15.2%, while a steep multi-year decline in state aid payments required major cuts to the city's workforce. For a city just regaining its financial footing, the tornado could have been a knockout blow. But we had different ideas.

As the city's top administrative and financial officer, my role was to track all expenditures—contractors, employee time, equipment, supplies, the whole works. But New England isn't exactly tornado alley, so we had no experience responding to a disaster of this type and of this scale, and neither did the Massachusetts Emergency Management Agency (MEMA). What's more, a wave of vendors previously unknown to us flew in from all corners of the country, insisting that we were obligated to use them for storm recovery operations. They ruffled more than a few feathers in City Hall. Meanwhile, damage estimates were adding up to millions of dollars. As just one example, the former State Armory in Springfield sustained damage that was estimated at $4.5 million. To top it off, FEMA and MEMA started to deny some of our claims. We were authorizing expenditures of millions of dollars, unsure if we'd ever recoup a penny in reimbursements.

Without prior experience in disaster recovery at this scale, and without sufficient time to research and review each of the damage assessments in depth, it became clear the city needed outside expertise to navigate the maze of federal and state regulations that drive disaster recovery funding. Through an official bid procurement process, Springfield hired Resilire Engineering and Consulting, LLC, to help us navigate the FEMA Public Assistance Program. Josh Norman of Resilire had spent years in New Orleans working for cities and towns affected by Hurricane Katrina. He and his team knew FEMA's rules and regulations inside and out. In fact, one of the major victories for our city was when FEMA approved our request to reevaluate the original damage estimate for the State Armory building: An updated analysis showed it was more cost-effective to replace the facility rather than repair it. So, using FEMA guidance, and with the help of Resilire, the city submitted an updated request for a full replacement and FEMA agreed, increasing available funds up from the original $4.5 million to $18 million.

It was a similar story for the former Alfred G. Zanetti School building. The district had vacated that site two years before the tornado, relocating the school and at the time was using the building as a storage facility. FEMA's initial determination called for zero reimbursement dollars. However, we successfully argued that the building was a swing space and FEMA awarded us an additional $7 million reimbursement, bringing our total to $25 million.

It was then that we realized the incredible opportunity in front of us. It was only logical: Residents would not be best served simply by restoring damaged buildings to their former condition. Instead, these FEMA dollars represented an extraordinary opportunity to invest in our communities in ways we had never previously had the financial means to do. Springfield partnered with MEMA to apply for entry into a FEMA pilot program (part of the Sandy Recovery Improvement

Act of 2013) that would allow us to reallocate recovery funds—like the $7 million for the empty Zanetti building (which was ultimately sold for $1.5 million to MGM Springfield as part of the site designated for the new casino opened in 2018)— toward projects in other locations. This was a pivotal moment for our city's recovery and future renaissance.

FEMA approved our request to put the funding toward five important projects for the city: an $800,000 parent and community center operated by Springfield Schools (opened in 2013); the $4.2 million renovation and expansion of an environmental education center in Springfield's largest park to support our schools' ECOS outdoor learning program (completed in 2016); a new $10.2 million facility for Springfield's South End Community Center (opened in 2017); $14.2 million in major renovations to a former U.S. Army reserve center, converted by Springfield Police for training, youth evaluation, and evidence storage and renamed the Paul J. Fenton Public Safety Annex (completed in 2017); and the new $12.8 million Raymond A. Jordan Senior Center (opened in 2018). In the end, through the hard work of city employees, collaboration with state and federal partners, and financial and labor insights generated by our city's integrated management systems, Springfield was on the hook to provide only a small fraction—just 13%—of this $97 million rebuilding effort.

Let me emphasize that the process to secure these reimbursements involved more than simply relying on best practices. We were successful because of the systems we had in place ahead of time that provided real-time visibility into labor spending. This data was critical. With it, we secured the greatest amount of FEMA reimbursements available to us—funding that has made it possible to restore our city and revive our neighborhoods.

★ ★ ★

Sadly, the tornado wasn't the only tumultuous event in Springfield around that time. In 2011, a major ice storm caused critical damage to parts of our infrastructure, and an October snowstorm caused additional setbacks. (However, guided by our newfound expertise in handling these situations properly, we recovered $17.6 million in federal assistance related to these events.) Then in 2012, we suffered a natural gas explosion just blocks away from where 10,000 spectators had gathered hours earlier for Springfield's day-after Thanksgiving parade. It happened just as a tree-lighting ceremony was taking place in the Quadrangle near Metro Center, where hundreds of onlookers felt the impact. For many of us, there was an uneasy wave of *déjà vu*. On that frigid day, when people needed warm shelter, we huddled with leaders from Health & Human Services, building inspectors, first responders, and Columbia Gas. Once again, we made decisions that would impact the people of Springfield, and once again were blessed to have tremendous partners and contractors on our side. Businesses reopened and residents were rehoused. The fact is, adversity reveals character, and people throughout the city rose to the occasion as we knew they would.

In the years since the 2011 tornado, Springfield has seen its economy recover substantially and its fiscal position improve. While the majority of development projects within the city have been funded by the private sector, securing additional federal, state, and local funding has helped us complete a number of ambitious recovery projects and contributed to our citywide revival. In January 2016 for example, the U.S. Housing Department awarded Springfield $17 million in funding through its National Disaster Resilience Competition (NDRC) to be used for innovative projects that would further increase our resilience and attract more investment. This award also leveraged $80.2 million from outside sources to fund projects throughout Springfield, including rebuilding one of several Springfield dams; creating a new source of solar power for one of our elementary schools that serves as a shelter during disasters; the launch of Springfield Healthy Homes, a program that funds housing rehabilitation in the Memorial Square and Six Corners neighborhoods; and the creation of the Springfield Innovation Center, which helps to equip low-income residents with the skills they need to work on projects being funded through the NDRC grant.

Having seen Springfield through both natural and man-made disasters, Mayor Sarno will be remembered for his focus on resiliency and preparedness. His dedication to moving the city forward—including investing disaster recovery funds in areas that would create the greatest amount of impact for our communities— helped to mitigate the damage of otherwise crippling blows to Springfield's finances in the wake of these disasters.

Managing Springfield's Largest Operational Cost: Our Workforce

To truly understand what's happening in any organization or process—and to improve it—we have long lived by the Woodward and Bernstein adage: "Follow the money." And in any and every municipality, as well as in many private enterprises, the money is in payroll.

Like most mid-sized cities, labor costs represent the lion's share of Springfield's budget. In fiscal year 2020 (July 1, 2019 through June 30, 2020), salary and benefits accounted for 68% of our nearly $698.9 million adopted budget. But for too many years, Springfield was unable to follow the money. That's because prior to the 2009 implementation of our UKG workforce management system, we were trapped by a series of paper-based timesheets and punch cards and were using Microsoft Excel spreadsheets to track labor expenses. Worse, each of our 30 departments had its *own* payroll staff, making it virtually impossible to aggregate city-wide data. We could only infrequently perform basic spot-check audits using data that was months old. Also, we had no analytical tools to find trends and take corrective actions. That meant payroll errors went undetected and there were no checks and balances regarding the use of vacation and sick time.

We knew that significant gaps, lapses, and abuses of the system were present, but we just didn't know where or didn't have the data to back up our questions. We also didn't have real-time data, so, for example, we wouldn't see an employee's accumulated paid time off... until the employee retired and a large accrued payout was due. In fact, a decade after implementing the UKG system, we continue to uncover and resolve problems. Take the Police Department's "balance of overtime" provision for example. It works like this: If an officer's shift normally ends at 6 p.m., but the officer must remain on site for an incident or to complete an arrest of a suspect, s/he is typically awarded overtime for the balance of that shift, which is intended to be paid out upon the officer's next promotion. However, we were seeing massive payouts for retiring officers—this had essentially become a *de facto* (and unchecked) system for stashing away large sums of retirement money. When the amounts reached the city's main ledger, there was no breakdown of the underlying details—only a (very large) number representing the amount due. Taking a closer look in recent years, we found that officers were being compensated for a career's worth of these "balance of overtime" payouts at the time of retirement, and at their most senior pay rate. That explained why an audit conducted in fiscal 2020 revealed that we are carrying a $3.7 million liability for all accrued liabilities, and a liability of $1.3 million in "balance of overtime" payouts.

It is legacy processes, systems, and situations like this that led us to the 30-year employee who almost never reported vacation or sick time. That's how we ended up with runaway overtime costs and inefficient deployment of full- and part-time employees. With more paid school crossing guards than we had school crossing locations. And employees accruing vacation balances far greater than what they were contractually entitled to. The paper problems extended to our benefits and pension programs as well. A lack of automated reconciliation processes resulted in mismanagement of payroll deductions, inefficient internal controls, and inconsistent data.

Difficulties were especially acute in our School Department. Millions of dollars earmarked for infrastructure were instead allocated to operating expenses, which meant that buildings were falling into serious disrepair following years of neglect. Wages were frozen, contract negotiations were stalled, there was little money for books and supplies, and hundreds of teachers and paraprofessionals were leaving for other jobs in nearby school districts. Those who remained posted shockingly low attendance rates.

After taking office in 2008, Mayor Sarno moved swiftly to address the situation at large. He understood that automation and data analytics would provide real-time visibility into citywide spending and could be the key to finally gaining a handle on our workforce and payroll challenges. After all, you can't manage what you can't see, and you need a plan to attain that vision. Springfield's deployment of the automated workforce management system from UKG represents one of the early, primary initiatives in this effort to gain control of our costs. The system includes several key components:

- **Electronic timekeeping:** Since labor is our city's most controllable expense, we were eager to see the details that had long been obscured. The automated workforce management system helps us track employee time and attendance so we can better manage workforce spending.
- **Absence management:** This toolset gave us visibility into trends around planned, incidental, and extended absences. It's enabled us to meet our budgets and forecasts and deploy our workforce more efficiently.
- **Workforce analytics:** Accumulating real-time data has allowed us to create analyses and reports that highlight extraordinary insights, and has empowered us to become better stewards of taxpayer dollars.

In addition, we integrated this system with our HR management and payroll systems and began to access it all from laptops and tablet devices. For an organization that was only recently using typewriters and index cards to create and store data, this was a tremendous leap forward in just a short period of time.

At the risk of overstating things, this deployment was a transformative experience for just about everyone in our city's government. We centralized city and school payroll teams into a single citywide payroll department with a combined staff sharing processes and information for all 6,300 city employees. (And through attrition, we eliminated five positions within the combined department.) We embedded the work rules from our contracts with 24 separate unions representing employees in the School Department as well as other areas like public works and public safety. The goal was to reduce errors (and abuses, which we still come across to this day), ensure every represented employee was paid accurately, and remove subjective guesswork from the process.

Even as we literally saved millions of dollars within the first year of implementation, we also created no small amount of culture shock once we started to track data across the city. The impacts were rapid, meaningful, and widespread. From a broader perspective, we were able to redesign our staffing models and leverage more part-time jobs to more accurately represent the hours per week truly necessary to complete the required work. We also identified misused overtime costs and inflated accrual payouts, quickly finding areas where spending could be reduced or eliminated altogether. For example, although we have a firm policy that says employees may only accrue 1.5 times their annual allotment for vacation time (it's a "use it or lose it" policy), former paper timesheets largely depended on a self-reporting honor system that was ripe for abuse. We found employees nearing retirement who had accrued months of vacation time. By announcing their retirement date and then using that accrued time to go out on extended vacation, *while staying on payroll*, these employees would earn even more sick time and vacation time. This was a mind-blowing discovery. As soon as we could track the data, we saw every employee who exceeded that capped accrual limit, and we put an end to it.

Without question, this was a culture shock to finally hold employees accountable. So, to be fair, we created a policy to give them all one year to come into compliance. We essentially let them use up excess vacation time. After that, any employee exceeding the cap would no longer accrue additional vacation time. As a result, we made tremendous strides in managing our liabilities. We greatly reduced our legacy balances: Over a six-year period, the average sick accrual balance per employee in our schools was cut by a quarter. Payouts to terminated or retiring employees that previously entailed large sums of money declined to defensible, appropriate levels. As opportunities to abuse the system decline steadily, we predict these levels will remain favorable in the future.

Before implementing the UKG system, we were sure (but couldn't prove) that some people were not entering their sick time and vacation time when they were away, knowing that no one would be the wiser because there was no accountability or control. Now, we have checks and balances in place to prevent future "Cal Ripkens." Similarly, we have been able to use our new analytics tools to do a deeper analysis of employee absenteeism. We started by looking at month-to-month comparisons based on the type of absence—planned, unplanned, and extended—and were able to identify departments that had higher rates of absenteeism. Once we drilled into the details, we could see what was driving the outliers and the trends by examining the percentage of total hours absent and whether the absence was planned or unplanned. Now, we can even drill down to a specific employee, communicate with department heads, and gather critical information to determine: how long the individual will be out; whether we need to hire additional personnel to overcome a staffing gap, or simply use overtime; and whether the city is responsible for paying workers' compensation to the employee. These kinds of insights and corrective actions were simply unthinkable with our previous paper-based processes, lack of audit-ability, and highly variable rules and practices.

In one example, workforce analytics helped us identify a city employee (one who was responsible for paying bills and taking in cash) who was in fact stealing department money and high-priced items. When flat-screen TVs were delivered to the building, they'd mysteriously disappear. Department credit cards were used to buy gift cards and clothes. Previously, with no systems or controls in place, the employee happily took advantage. However following our investigation, we were able to uncover the thefts, and have since reclaimed that money.

In another money-saving example, under the auspices of the Department of Public Works (DPW), city-owned snowplows, trucks, and other vehicles are equipped with GPS navigation/tracking devices. That means we can continuously track the vehicle—and, hence, the driver. When we began to comb through that data, we saw far too many instances of waste, fraud, and abuse of taxpayer resources. We saw the DPW truck driver who was bringing mulch home for his own yard while still on the clock. We saw workers at home for four or five hours in the middle of the day. We saw DPW vehicles that were supposed to be at the transfer station were instead in another part of the city—or county. In addition, we saw snowplow drivers traversing the same streets and the same neighborhoods for hours at a time, solely to accumulate additional overtime hours. Needless to say, we were happy to uncover these situations and take strong corrective measures, which had the added benefit of future deterrence.

Another area of focus was custodial overtime that was classified as "controllable." The way our staffing was previously structured, we were using overtime to mask significant, systemic staffing problems. We were able to dig into the data and see the details—who, how, why, and when—to understand the situation and make important changes to our management processes and practices. That translated into a reduction of controllable overtime by 80%, which is roughly the equivalent of one full-time employee. We also reduced non-controllable overtime for tasks such as building inspections and alarm callbacks by 50%, largely by overhauling our staffing model to deploy more part-time employees. The total savings in salaries and overtime topped $900,000 in the first year.

Situations described here were rare, and our newfound visibility into the workforce enabled us to quickly identify and respond to them to eliminate sources of fraud and abuse of taxpayer dollars.

School Department Finances

The area where our workforce management initiatives had the greatest impact was in the 5,000-employee School Department and its sizeable budget managed by Pat Roach. It has surged from around $300 million in 2010 to more than $500 million in 2020. The data derived from our workforce management system gives Pat and his team clear and confident insights into the improvements that need to be made. Especially entering negotiations with teacher unions, this data is invaluable.

Just enrolling Springfield teachers into an electronic timekeeping system was an important milestone that enabled us to generate payroll checks more efficiently. Next, we tied the UKG system into our substitute management system, eSchool Solutions, to bring full accountability to absences. Teachers are instructed to use the system to self-report an absence and request a substitute teacher. Naturally, for each day a substitute teacher is required, there should be a corresponding sick day or other accrued leave for the missing teacher. But as Pat and his team started to perform daily audits, they uncovered more than $800,000 in uncharged teacher sick time—the rough equivalent of more than 20 full-time teacher salaries. Interestingly, once they began to track faculty absenteeism, the statistics for sick leave worsened as the numbers climbed. But that was no surprise—we were finally getting the absences properly captured and attributed. In a few months, once everyone was acclimated to the system, comfortable with the process, and aware of the central monitoring and the daily reports, those same statistics improved significantly.

Overall, this was an important issue to address because faculty absenteeism in any form has a direct impact on learning outcomes. While substitute teachers are an important contributor to the success of our schools, for each day a teacher is out, students fall behind due to the disruptive break in the learning cycle. Education suffers and costs increase. Fortunately, just as we had been able to do in other parts of the city budget, our newfound controls of inappropriate labor costs became a source of innovation and improvement for the School Department. For instance, Pat's team performed analyses on labor data and found there were many important opportunities to improve staff balance, performance, and efficiency. In some schools, custodians were understaffed and the schools relied on expensive overtime. Other schools were overstaffed. The UKG data helped to address these imbalances to reallocate the right custodial resources to the right places. The department also eliminated 68 central administrative positions (out of a total of 250) through attrition, layoffs, and transfers. In the first year, they reduced controllable overtime by 80%, saving hundreds of thousands of dollars.

Overtime expenses, which were once on a central budget, are now managed by the schools or, in some cases, by individual departments within the schools. When overtime spending hits their bottom line, as opposed to the district's shared budget, they notice. Now they are more likely to question and correct a staff imbalance or inefficiency. They are more careful with their spending and limited in what they will allow. It's a small change that has paid dividends over the years.

Most importantly, many of the savings generated by Springfield's new data-driven processes were being successfully reallocated into what really matters: improving educational outcomes for students. For starters, we hired more full-time academic intervention teachers to work closely with elementary school students struggling to read. By addressing these challenges early, we can improve student outcomes all the way through high school, so this change was particularly important and is now firmly part of the School Departments' operating budget. We also made the strategic decision to provide each student with a take-home laptop beginning in second grade. Cost-cutting labor insights created the seed money for the initiative, and each academic year since 2015–16 we have provisioned and distributed 22,000 laptops at an annual recurring cost of $5 million. When you consider that many of our families don't have computers at home, this is an important initiative for our district.

But what's the net-net for any public school system? Inarguably it has to be graduation rates and test scores, which in prior years were dismal. The 2007 student dropout rate for Springfield Schools (9.7%) was nearly three times the Massachusetts average. And in 2010, 11 of the city's 44 schools were determined by state education regulators to be chronically underperforming—in other words, failing. While it's difficult to unequivocally say that optimized labor costs directly equate to better academic performances, the circumstantial evidence is quite strong. Since the advent of these many financially strategic initiatives, our district's five-year graduation rate has soared, reaching 79% in 2019, and our dropout rate fell to an all-time low. More kids are finishing high school, just as every one of our elementary schools has marked notable performance improvements. More students are achieving better scores on state standardized tests, and more students are going on to pursue college, professional trades, and military service with a much-improved educational foundation from our public schools.

★ ★ ★

On a variety of fronts and from a variety of perspectives, Springfield's investments in workforce management and labor analytics have played a crucial role in the turnaround of our city. Again, that's not surprising since labor consumes such a large share of our budget. As bank robber Willie Sutton might say: *you focus there, because that's where the money is.* But the added benefit here is that the improvements were not one-time events. The processes, discipline, and more careful stewardship we implemented continue to yield cost savings that endure on an ongoing basis. By creating this positive financial momentum, we put ourselves in a position to take bolder action to improve Springfield in ways that allow us to provide better services to residents—which is why we're in business.

Keeping Public Safety a Top Priority

W hile it is extremely important to root out the waste, fraud, and abuse of taxpayer dollars and restore citizens' confidence in city government, it's equally important to make good choices with those savings. Springfield is funding projects that will improve the vital areas of public safety, education, economic vitality, local neighborhoods, and fiscal and operational excellence. Our Capital Improvement Plan provides the roadmap for these improvements and future capital spending.

In Springfield, collaboration has been the key to making the right decisions that have created such a lasting impact on our community. That's why, with our technology foundation firmly in place in 2013, the Springfield Office of Management and Budget (OMB) emerged as a consolidation of the city's finance departments together with my CAFO function. The office was formed by the Mayor and myself to bring an even deeper level of analytics and data-driven decision-making to the entire city. It effectively replaced Springfield's former CitiStat Department (based on a methodology used by the New York Police Department), which was formed under the auspices of the Finance Control Board. CitiStat wasn't perfect, but it did a good job of aggregating meaningful data—time and attendance, finance metrics, thresholds, milestones, and more—that allowed us to hold departments accountable and optimize the city's performance. The OMB has similar goals, though today we employ a much more collegial and collaborative style and are committed to funding projects that will improve the vital areas of education, economic vitality, and public safety.

Negotiating a New Police Contract

It was no surprise that once the city had its finances in order the Mayor decided to make public safety a high priority. Using OMB strategies, he allocated a significant portion of the savings we had generated from optimizing our labor budget for the purpose of providing resources to various public safety departments and was ultimately able to fund a 14% increase in police salaries over four years. This was a high priority; it was an opportunity to obtain meaningful cooperation in several key areas that had previously been the basis of ongoing disagreement with our police union. In exchange for this raise, we negotiated a new contract that encompasses a residency requirement for newly hired officers, a full-scale implementation of body-worn cameras, Narcan use by officers (who are typically first to the scene, ahead of EMTs), and a social media policy—referred to by the mayor as "the Big 4."

C3 Policing

We felt strongly that by requiring all police officers to live within city limits for the first 10 years of their tenure, it would enable them to create and maintain better relations with the people they serve, to align their interests more tightly with their own community, and give them a greater stake in policing outcomes and general quality of life. It would also enhance Springfield's property-tax base, strengthen our school enrollments, and enable our C3 policing strategy.

Counter Criminal Continuum Policing—what we call C3 policing—is a strategy first pioneered by Springfield Police in 2009. It's based on counter-insurgency methods used by U.S. Army Special Forces and adapted for use by civilian law enforcement. During his routine patrols in Springfield, a Massachusetts state trooper and 25-year Special Forces veteran theorized that the principles he and his fellow soldiers employed in Iraq might be equally useful in detecting, disrupting, and dismantling gang activity in certain high-crime districts. We adapted that model and applied it to a select few hotspots in the city. Since then, C3 policing has gained quite a bit of attention from the media. It's been positively featured on CBS's "60 Minutes" and on the pages of *The New York Times*. According to Commissioner Clapprood, who formerly served as captain of Springfield's C3 units, it comes down to listening to citizens, hearing their problems, and developing their trust: It's community policing on steroids, and it works.

Today, our C3 officers attend "Coffee with Cops" sessions to meet their community. They frequent neighborhood block parties and local events as guests. They even hold an annual Easter Egg Hunt and Halloween Trunk or Treat event for families—and it pays off. We've started to change the tide and reverse decades-long crime trends and patterns. What's more, it also allows us to deploy fewer officers, even as our effectiveness increases.

Police Body-Worn Cameras

Another high-profile aspect of our bargaining agreement with the police union is the adoption of body-worn cameras by our patrol officers, which is largely funded by savings generated through our technology-supported cost controls. While some police unions are wary of the use of these devices, we see them as a way to not only encourage fair methods by our officers, but also protect our officers. Of course, acquiring 500 body-worn cameras and developing the proper training and procedures that accompany them was an expensive proposition. Commissioner Clapprood spearheaded a thorough analysis, careful testing, and transparent procurement process. We were determined to get all the details right, including factors such as battery performance, video storage, reliability, and durability. In fact, our testers threw, dropped, and even shot at body cameras as part of their assessment. We also proceeded slowly with developing the policies and procedures for turning the cameras on and off. There are considerations with respect to privacy, juveniles, and healthcare facilities that need careful definition and explanation.

Ultimately, Springfield invested $4.4 million and began the test implementation in 2019. An additional grant of $1.1 million from the U.S. Justice Department helped facilitate the rollout even further. As of early 2021, Springfield police are equipped with body-worn cameras.

Real-time Crime Analysis

Even before we turned our attention to body-worn cameras, Springfield demonstrated a very clear commitment to supporting our police department, opening a state-of-the-art real-time crime analysis center in 2018. Overseen by a civilian director, this $1 million centralized facility on the second floor of police headquarters on Pearl Street represents the next generation in public safety. Technicians can merge and comb through video streams, perform instant record searches, and use sophisticated software to address incidents, assist officers, and help resolve situations as they happen. For instance, if police are looking for a green car, technicians can filter footage to remove cars of every other color. Or if they are searching for a pedestrian, the software can filter out all cars.

The department already has access to nearly 300 camera feeds—a mixture of public and private cameras from schools, government offices, local businesses, and even private citizens. The system can also tie into criminal records and databases and even social media feeds to search for and analyze potential threatening messages. ShotSpotter, a system that detects the distinctive sound of gunshots by triangulating sound patterns captured on strategically placed microphones, provides another layer of data that can be relayed to field officers. Before they even arrive at the scene, officers have a much more complete picture of the situation and can respond more effectively.

The cost of introducing real-time crime analysis in Springfield was nearly $1.3 million, which accounts for new software, hardware, personnel, and radio upgrades. And the benefits are vast: We have evolved and enhanced our policing abilities (and continue to do so), raised the profile of Springfield Police, and are better equipped to serve the public and protect our officers.

Recruitment & Retention

Recruitment and retention in public safety is a major challenge across the country. In Springfield, we've seen a 90% drop in the number of candidates taking the cadet test and seeking admission to our police academy. Where we previously had 500–600 people take the cadet test, we now see only 50–60. With an average of 40–50 vacant positions at a given time, the inability to fill these positions forces the department to rely on expensive overtime shifts to fill the gaps. Not only is this financially disadvantageous, such a strategy risks overworking our officers.

However, our police force is headed in the right direction. Commissioner Clapprood—elevated to her post in 2019 after 40 years on the force—has boosted morale, stabilized the department, and brought refreshing levels of accountability. Even during tough times, Mayor Sarno has been an unwavering supporter of Springfield's first responders. Although we have reduced payroll by eliminating vacant positions, we have never once laid off a police officer or firefighter.

Candidly, there have been occasions where the Mayor has pushed me out of my financial comfort zone to give our first responders the tools they need to succeed—and he has been absolutely correct to do so. Without question, our police force is in the best shape I have ever seen it.

Elevating the School Nutrition Experience:
A Unique City-School Partnership

When operating one of the largest school districts in the Commonwealth of Massachusetts—and the one with the highest poverty rate—you face a broader set of challenges in preparing your children for the future. The last thing we want is for these challenges to distract from our district's core mission: student success.

For years, escalating dropout rates, attendance and punctuality issues, disruptive behavior, and other factors were, frankly, undermining performance across Springfield Schools. District leaders found that one of the best strategies to reverse these unfavorable trends and refocus students on their educations was to remove barriers to learning. The fact is, however, that hungry, malnourished kids can't learn—and this was posing a barrier for far too many students across our district.

Harnessing federal funding, establishing corporate and industry partnerships, teaming with nonprofit organizations, and developing good old-fashioned community engagement, Springfield Schools—led by Superintendent Daniel J. Warwick since 2012—successfully introduced a range of nutrition programs that have reduced food insecurity while promoting sustainable and healthy nutrition for more than 30,000 students in 68 public and charter schools. And just as important, as our schools have rolled out these nutrition programs to serve as wrap-around supports for students, we have observed remarkable improvements from 2012 to 2020 across the district:

- Attendance and meal-participation rates have soared.
- Chronic truancy and absenteeism have dropped.
- In-school and out-of-school suspensions have decreased dramatically.

- School nurse visits due to hunger declined by 1,400 in one year, a 71% decline.
- Overall academic proficiency rose 8%.
- The district's dropout rate is 4.4%, an all-time low representing a 54% decrease since 2012.
- Graduation rates have climbed 17% district-wide, reaching as high as 85.6%, 89.6%, and 91.5% at our top three performing high schools. (In 2012, these schools were at 39.9%, 74.6%, and 71%, respectively.)

Although it's difficult to prove a cause-effect relationship, it's equally difficult to label our school nutrition programs as anything but a resounding success. But to gain a true understanding of how well these programs have performed, it's helpful to start with a clearer picture of Springfield Schools.

Springfield is Massachusetts's second largest school district (only Boston has more students) with a district-wide enrollment of about 25,000 and 5,000 employees working in nearly 60 public schools. In the 2019–20 school year, 67.1% of students were Hispanic, 18.9% were African American, 9.7% were Caucasian, and Asian and other ethnicities made up the remaining balance. More than three-quarters of these students are considered economically disadvantaged, making ours the second poorest school district in Massachusetts. This partly reflects a citywide unemployment rate that is roughly twice the state average. Since 77.6% of Springfield students are eligible for free meals on the basis of family income, the district implemented the Community Eligibility Provision (CEP) in 2015–16 to provide free breakfast and lunch to all students who want them, regardless of income.

Since its enactment in 2010, the national CEP program has allowed schools with sufficiently high rates of free and reduced-price meal eligibility to provide meals to *all* students at no charge. Schools generally see reduced administrative costs through CEP when breakfast and lunch are free to all students and no money changes hands. That's certainly been the case in Springfield: Although our city has invested significant resources in improving the school meal experience through numerous programs, our finances have not suffered. That's because when more children participate in the programs—and in Springfield Schools, participation is high—the district receives greater government reimbursements, so our school nutrition revenue increases.

More students today are enjoying nutritious and balanced meals that include fresh fruits and vegetables, milk, and whole grains. In many cases in our relatively low-income school district, these meals account for a significant amount of the students' calories and nutrients over an entire day, making up the difference between food-insecure and well-nourished. With full stomachs, students are able to focus on learning instead of appetites. Although officials are quick to say that multiple factors are involved, objective measures of academic performance in our schools are on the rise.

* * *

On a variety of fronts, Springfield is leading the way on a national basis with a range of school nutrition programs for which the district now tracks dramatically favorable results. Of course, in a large urban school district, daily meal operations are a major undertaking, and key relationships—like the district's decade-long partnership with the New England Dairy & Food Council—have helped. But no other partner has made an impact in Springfield Schools quite like Sodexo.

Springfield partnered with the food service management company in 2005, around the time the Finance Control Board took charge and after an assessment determined that in comparison to other districts our school meal programs could be doing much better—nutritionally *and* financially. Sodexo was brought in to help our schools put a plan in place to significantly improve on all aspects—from meal participation to labor control—and report in detail on how the overarching program is operating. Effective immediately, all cafeteria staff reported into Sodexo, a decision that not only created a more defined career path for food service employees but also allowed the organization to more fluidly move staff from one school or facility to another. This was important, because as the team from Sodexo scrutinized labor costs (leveraging the same UKG workforce management system as the city to calculate labor hours per meal), they found some schools' costs were significantly higher than others. That spurred some good old-fashioned cost accounting and led to staff reallocations and uniform improvements—all of which yielded cost savings that were redirected right back into our district's food programs.

From the start, Sodexo was on the hook to turn around a $2 million deficit and their team delivered, exceeding the organization's commitment to Springfield. Together, we accomplished a series of very ambitious goals. On the school side, Pat Roach gets the credit. In any scenario where there are many constituencies to appease, you need leaders who are aligned and committed to a vision. It's Team-work 101, and Pat has been the driving force behind transformational improve-ments that our city desperately needed—improvements that, by all counts, are quite groundbreaking.

Breakfast in the Classroom

In the early years of partnering with the district, Sodexo built out the much-needed infrastructure our schools would require in order to take our nutrition programs to the next level. As the city recovered in a broad sense, Sodexo and the School Department were able to think more creatively about how to increase student participation. The key, they decided, was to look at school nutrition as more than simply a federal compliance. Although we were already offering free breakfast for all in our cafeterias each morning, participation was shockingly low at only 20%. The solution that Sodexo piloted in 2015—which has become our School Depart-ment's flagship initiative—was "Breakfast in the Classroom," a model that's been implemented districtwide across all grade levels since 2018.

Breakfast in the Classroom rewrote the rules for how school meals are con-sumed: Our students eat breakfast at their desks during first period, which counts as instruction time, and as a result, districtwide participation has surged to 80%. In addition to offering breakfast at no cost, the food is very accessible—no one is miss-ing a meal if they arrive to school late. Best of all, following breakfast, the students are well-nourished and in a far better position to focus on the day's schoolwork.

At the start of the implementation, the district piloted Breakfast in the Class-room in one school: Brightwood Elementary School, serving 350 students. There, they dealt with both expected resistance and unexpected hurdles. This school was selected initially because there was a higher percentage of students who live below the poverty line and we felt the program would be well-received—and it was. The School Department subsequently began to roll out the program in three waves: first to the schools that were eager to participate, then schools that were initially lukewarm but willing participants once they saw the results from early adopters, and finally we finished up with the laggard schools that were understandably con-cerned about issues such as loss of instruction time, messy desks, and classroom trashcans filled with food waste. Over three years, we phased in all 60 of our schools, averaging 20 schools per year.

Joao Alves, who has been a teacher and administrator at Roger L. Putnam Vocational Technical Academy for many years, explained that Breakfast in the Classroom succeeded because school leaders steadily responded to the initial challenges. For instance, at Putnam, we obviously cannot have students eating breakfast near oil, wood chips, or metal filings, so we had to move people around. "There was some pushback from teachers at first," Alves noted. "But by the second full year, the hurdles were gone, and we'd worked out the kinks. Everyone is on board now. These changes didn't just happen. The school district's leadership put the right people in the right places—they deserve the credit. We're fortunate to have a very high graduation rate, and initiatives like this are surely making an impact."

It was no small achievement to get all school administrators to participate—and get the students on board as well. Springfield's Breakfast in the Classroom wouldn't have worked without the complete support of Mayor Sarno and Superintendent Warwick. They saw the value of this program at an early stage and created the supportive environment that helped it succeed. The program has since drawn attention and praise throughout the community. In April 2017, Duron Harmon—a member of the New England Patriots at the time—presented a $22,000 grant at Springfield's High School of Commerce, which was a big hit in our sports-enthused community. Central High School—the first high school in Massachusetts to implement a breakfast program like this—earned the Healthy Start Award from the Eos Foundation, as well as a grant from the Community Foundation of Western Massachusetts. These grants provided support for additional equipment purchases and other administrative costs.

With the program firmly implemented across every one of our schools by 2018, we've seen academic performance increase, tardiness decrease, attendance go up, behavior issues improve, and nurse visits go down. It's hard to argue with such outcomes. But for all the innovation and investment taking place in Springfield Schools, the success of our food programs still comes down to our ability to serve nutritious meals that appeal to the students. The best measure for this is what the experts call average daily participation (ADP)—the percentage of enrolled students who eat lunch or breakfast at school on any given day. In Springfield, we've far surpassed the national rates, and schools that introduced Breakfast in the Classroom are big drivers of our gains. Before rolling out the program, Central

High School's lunch ADP was relatively high at 73%, but breakfast was only 25%—well below the national average. By October 2016, however, just one year after adopting the Breakfast in the Classroom model Central's breakfast ADP was 87%, which is 3.5 times its ADP from just two years earlier. That's also 2.9 times the national breakfast average. In other words, by focusing on food quality and student needs, as well as taking advantage of federal programs and nonprofit grants, we are bringing more food to more kids than ever before.

Soon, the question circulating around the School Department became: "How do we get to 90% participation?" Turning their focus from accessibility to nutrition, the schools and Sodexo figured out a way to improve the quality of the foods we served our kids.

Culinary & Nutrition Center

The foundation of our district's success with Breakfast in the Classroom was the driver of one of our most ambitious moves: the $21 million Culinary and Nutrition Center (CNC) that opened in 2019 and has already generated a $1.3 million efficiency that is being reinvested into further improving school meals. This 62,000-square-foot facility is fully managed by Sodexo and is truly the heart and soul of our many school nutrition programs.

We were already serving all kids universal free meals, but the CNC has empowered Springfield Schools to expand a scratch-made cooking model that can accommodate students' demands for greater variety. When we first implemented Breakfast in the Classroom, for example, we started out serving basics like cereal or prepackaged muffins, but the CNC enabled us to expand and improve our menus. Now, our schools are serving scratch-made options: freshly chopped fruit, house-made muffins, fresh egg sandwiches, and our own yogurt. Still in the early days of operating the CNC, these breakfast options are available two days a week (with prepackaged items still offered on the off-days), though by 2024 we anticipate that house-made foods will be served 5 days a week. In the meantime, Sodexo is excitedly working to tweak the foods, finetune the recipes, and introduce new kid-friendly options while leveraging healthy ingredients. Rather than replace cooking in the individual schools, the CNC supports scratch cooking and provides menu components that are transported by Sodexo staff to school facilities where they undergo final preparation. If student participation and nourishment are the most important factors, then increasing the quality of foods that kids like to eat, and making these foods accessible to all, is a win-win.

In a sign of our ambitions, the CNC was designed to accommodate our district's projected growth. With no shortage of ideas—internally and from the community—around what this facility can be and what it can provide, the schools created an advisory committee of involved parents, business leaders, and advocacy organizations to provide guidance. Their involvement has translated to actual improvement for our schools and the community. There's a lot of talk about eating local and bringing nutrition into schools, and all of us feel very proud that we are making it a reality for our students. Springfield Schools and Sodexo implemented an adopt-a-farm program, partnering with five farms in Western Massachusetts's Pioneer Valley to source local produce, bread, milk, and fresh ingredients. Sodexo sets annual purchasing goals, meets with farmers, and suggests the best crops to plant to meet our schools' needs. They develop the school menus and the meals are made from scratch at the CNC. For instance, we can serve our students pasta or lasagna topped with sauce made from local produce. In short, we've made it very easy to provide the nourishment our students need to learn and grow.

Beyond fresher ingredients and more appealing menus, the CNC fosters a positive learning environment. Like many school districts around the country, we are eager to teach students more about where their food comes from and about the benefits of local sourcing. So, in addition to the adopt-a-farm program, dozens of schools across the district have started their own vegetable gardens where students can help grow what they consume. In many cases, this has been integrated into the curricula. The vegetables are harvested, channeled to the CNC to be washed and prepared, and served in each building's cafeteria, with online menus identifying which foods incorporate the school's own harvest.

Before the CNC got up and running, John F. Kennedy Middle School—one of the first schools to serve its own garden vegetables in the cafeteria—had to ship its produce to a facility in Rhode Island to be washed and cleaned, then shipped back to the school. With the new culinary center and a new streamlined process, today more than 13,000 Springfield students attend schools that incorporate garden-grown ingredients into student meals.

To help manage these farm-to-school programs (as well as our composting, recycling, and other initiatives), the district hired a full-time director of sustainability. Sodexo, too, has established its own company-centered goals for sustainability within the district. Whether it's composting or installing the next school garden, the focus on sustainable nutrition in Springfield schools is a serious commitment.

On this front, we are well-aligned with one of the CNC's largest sponsors. Since 2017, the Henry P. Kendall Foundation has been a major contributor to the success of our culinary center. The foundation is committed to creating a healthy and sustainable food system in New England, and for decades has partnered with institutions like ours to support the local growing movement and increase opportunities for local and regional suppliers. An initial $35,000 grant from the Kendall Foundation allowed Springfield Schools to hire a consultant to assist in developing a plan for procurement, processing, and meal guidelines to be incorporated into the launch and operation of the CNC. Then in 2018, we received a $275,000 two-year grant to help initiate, develop, and sustain meaningful student and community engagement programs through the CNC, and in 2019 received an additional $50,000 to support a comprehensive staff training program. This is all seed money. As participation across our schools increases, our school nutrition programs will become more sustainable and the impact of our work will reach well beyond any single initiative.

Tackling Food Insecurity

Sodexo's staff produces and packages numerous foods to support all of our school meal programs, not just Breakfast in the Classroom. They partner with the district to run our farm-to-school programs, local purchasing and sustainability, a culinary arts training program for students and employees, and even provide catering services—which, in fact, we leveraged to cater the Mayor's 2019 inaugural gala at Putnam Vocational. Most importantly, together we are tackling food insecurity among students and their families, with Sodexo overseeing a handful of initiatives that provide for our kids when they're not at school.

We recognize that our universal free breakfast and lunch programs are the primary food source for many. It's our goal to fill in the gaps so that students don't go home hungry at night, over the weekend, or in the summertime. To help, several schools offer in-school evening meals for students through the Child and Adult Care Food Program. The district also partnered with the Food Bank of Western Massachusetts to fill backpacks for approximately 250 eligible students to take home on weekends. It's a program that's partially funded by Sodexo employees and others in the district who contribute small monthly donations via payroll deductions, and through funding from Blue Cross Blue Shield, Health New England, and Jeff's Granola—all of which have made it possible for us to distribute high-quality meals throughout the school year. Finally, our summer food service program provides free meals to children and teenagers over the summer vacation. In 2019, we had 47 school sites involved and offering meals under the program. It's a terrific initiative helping families cope with the rising costs of food and other necessities.

Evaluating our district's progress over time, it's become clear that removing *all* critical barriers to learning requires a multipronged approach in order to meet the many different needs of Springfield's community: from making nutritious foods more accessible to students, to removing the stigma of free school meals, to addressing food insecurity on non-school days, and connecting kids with local and regional farmers.

Beyond Meals: The Learning Connection

Of course, the primary objective of any school is to improve learning outcomes and encourage student success. In recent years, Springfield has seen concurrent improvements in several metrics regarding student behavior and well-being. Quite rightly, our school officials are careful not to assert that the surge in school meal programs is the only factor involved in these improvements. However, they are equally reluctant to dismiss the correlations as coincidence. From their perspective, nutrition programs have made a difference by reducing hunger and improving students' temperament during the school day and making them more ready to learn. Superintendent Warwick is quick to address the bottom-line impact: "These meals are getting more people to school—consistently and on time. That right there is improving our academic outcomes."

While more research is needed, data from inner-city middle school students in Boston suggests that a universal free breakfast program was associated with lower parental reports of food insufficiency and increased attendance. And in analyzing Springfield's data for truancy and chronic absenteeism for 2011–12 (before implementation) vs. 2015–16 (the first year of implementation), we observed that those rates fell 1.8 and 1.5 percentage points, respectively. During the same period, the combined number of in-school and out-of-school suspensions fell by 45%, and student arrests and bullying incidents fell 53%. Visits to the school nurse from children feeling hungry fell 23%, from 2,047 in 2015 to 1,577 in 2017. Also, when Breakfast in the Classroom was introduced, punctuality improved notably: It used to take three bells to get students to the classroom, but now they're there before the first bell rings.

"It's really important that kids get nutritious meals every day, and in our community, we've really worked awfully hard to make that possible for all our kids," Warwick said. "All the research supports how important that is for the kids from a health standpoint. It's also very important for learning."

Naturally this is significant in an era when there is a heavy emphasis on academic testing, and the following is undeniable: Since introducing Breakfast in the Classroom, our graduation rates increased 17%; overall academic proficiency rose 8%; and proficiency in specific subjects also rose—from a modest 1% increase in science to an 11% proficiency increase in mathematics. In 2019, 363 fewer students dropped out compared to 2012: a 54% decline.

* * *

What did we learn? Well, many things. Pat and I learned that synergies between the city and the School Department matter. We learned the importance of improving our logistics, building relationships with vendors, and ensuring everyone knows the school protocols. We learned about the importance of buy-in and leadership—from school district administrators to principals to teachers to students and families. When you have leadership aligned, it's amazing what can get accomplished.

Turning school meals into shared community experiences has obvious benefits for low-income children, but may also help their more advantaged peers in ways that are difficult to measure: a greater sense of shared social goods; an enhanced understanding of how nutrition can tie us all together; or even just a few minutes sharing a meal with someone from a different neighborhood, ethnicity, or life history. To me, these are important benefits for the entire City of Springfield and can be a model for other cities nationwide.

An Urban Renaissance in Springfield:
Western New England's Place to Live, Work, and Play

If there's an overarching lesson to take away from Springfield and its historic financial turnaround, it's this: Perseverance pays. The fact is, when our city reluctantly fell under the control of the Finance Control Board in 2004, it was the culmination of decades of bad decisions, bad circumstances, and, yes, some bad luck. The decline of the manufacturing sector and the near-total erasure of blue-collar jobs throughout the latter half of the 20th century had gutted many once vibrant cities and left them struggling financially. Springfield was not immune to these trends. It took many years to reach that low point, and we realized that it would take many more years to pull ourselves out of it.

When Domenic J. Sarno took the reins as mayor in 2008, he devised a citywide implementation blueprint to frame up a top-down commitment to economic development, financial stewardship, and community-based programs to improve the quality of life for our citizens, education for our children, and public safety for all residents and visitors alike. The blueprint facilitated development opportunities throughout the city and worked to solidify Springfield as the center of the region's convention, meeting, and entertainment initiatives. It also supported opportunities for net new market-rate housing development, efforts to attract new businesses and employment, and even Springfield's marketing and rebranding. Altogether, it was a bold plan to reclaim our standing as both an economic force in western New England and a thriving city in which to live, work, and play.

Those of us serving the city for more than a decade as part of Mayor Sarno's administration have seen Springfield make tremendous progress. Goals that had been on our to-do list for many, many years became feasible for the first time. Using just $50 million in city funds, we completed $350 million of direct improvements across a wide portfolio of projects, such as a new community center, senior center, transportation venues, and more. Some of our signature developments have included a $95 million railcar factory, the $94 million restoration of Springfield Union Station, and the construction of Massachusetts's first full-scale casino—the $960 million MGM Springfield complex. All told, we've seen $4.5 billion in economic development—an unsurpassed level of investment in the city's vitality.

Previously, the prevailing attitude was, "Well, you can't do *that* in Springfield." Today? We are driven by a can-do spirit—one that starts with, "Why *not* Springfield?" People are moving to Springfield. Residents are keeping their children enrolled in our public schools. Businesses want to invest in Springfield. Students want to attend college in Springfield. Visitors from across the region come to Springfield to enjoy our many recreational and cultural attractions. In countless ways, Springfield is transforming into a thriving destination—the kind of city that my colleagues and I have always envisioned.

The Place to Live

One of the pillars of a thriving city is its ability to attract people to its various neighborhoods, and across the city we have seen strong demand for residential apartments, condominiums, and houses. Springfield's real estate market has blossomed, with many homes reaching unprecedented prices in the $200,000–300,000 range. We are building nicer homes, with higher property values and higher tax revenues. We've encouraged developers to build market-rate housing, i.e., apartments that do not carry rent ceilings or other price restrictions. This is an attractive proposition for developers, who are responding to the opportunities on several fronts.

In August 2020, the long-awaited construction project to redevelop the former Court Square Hotel at 31 Elm Street finally began. It sits across the way from Springfield City Hall and is one of the city's oldest historic gems. The $52 million development project represents a public/private partnership in the truest sense, bringing us closer with key allies like Massachusetts Gov. Charlie Baker, Springfield's own Peter Picknelly of OPAL Real Estate, WinnCompanies of Boston, MassMutual CEO Roger Crandall, leadership from MGM Springfield, and many others. With their support, this landmark revitalization project, which promises to convert the 30-year abandoned structure into 74 residential units plus 12,000 square feet of commercial space, will bring us closer to completing the transformation of our downtown district. It's a transformation that is ultimately made possible because we got our finances under control all those years ago.

All told, from an economic development perspective, it's projects like this that are building excitement and gaining the attention of people who are taking a closer look at all that Springfield has to offer. But it's just one of many.

Motorcycle enthusiasts know that Springfield was the renowned home of Indian Motorcycle Company, a prestigious brand born in 1901. Today, developers are in the process of restoring that legendary factory building in the Mason Square neighborhood and converting it into 60 new residential units—a $35 million effort. And in Silverbrick Square, in the historic YMCA building, 99 existing apartments will be rehabilitated and an additional 15 units will be added—an $11 million undertaking in total. We've earmarked some of these apartments for Springfield teachers and provided them with below-market rents to attract and retain qualified faculty who can live in a professional cohort. Nearby, a $9 million project will add an additional 60 market-rate apartments, as well as a floor reserved for teachers, to the historic Willys-Overland Building, built in 1916. A few blocks away, a $40 million project is underway to completely renovate 489 units within four separate buildings at Chestnut Park Towers. The revamped complex will include a fitness center, resident community space, workforce development training center, children's playroom, and a computer lab. To no one's surprise, there is a waiting list to live there.

Altogether, Springfield will see the creation or renovation of hundreds of units of apartment and condominium housing—many of which will feature the historic flourishes and rustic aesthetic that call back to our city's rich history. But the revival of our communities has extended far beyond residential development. Our Riverfront Park has undergone a nearly $3 million facelift, including new lights, pedestrian walkways, a stage for outdoor concerts, lawn area, playground equipment, and a newly dedicated 9/11 memorial: a 9.5-foot monument that includes a piece of steel salvaged from the World Trade Center in Manhattan.

Further, with support from Gov. Baker and through a $3.5 million grant from the MassWorks Infrastructure Program, the state has helped to reinvigorate Pynchon Plaza. After years of vandalism and neglect, this vibrant community space, which connects our downtown to the Quadrangle and the Springfield Museums, is now reopened. Gov. Baker also came to Springfield's rescue after flooding in our Forest Park neighborhood forced road closures for many months and jeopardized Springfield's nationally renowned Bright Nights holiday lighting festival. With $3 million in state funding, we were able to repair the infrastructure, reopen the park's main entrance, and preserve this beloved holiday tradition.

Elsewhere, we've spent nearly $7 million to refresh some of Downtown Springfield's core thoroughfares: Central, Lyman, Main, Taylor, Union, and Worthington Streets. We've made landscaping and site improvements to Cross Street with new trees and tree wells, and added numerous crosswalks and sidewalk improvements. Stearns Square is undergoing a $1.8 million facelift with new landscaping and paving, as well as sidewalk extensions to accommodate and promote outdoor dining. There's even a year-round weekly farmers market in Downtown Springfield for the first time in years.

At the same time, we are investing in several areas to increase public safety (e.g., through the introduction of C3 policing, among other measures) and improve transportation. We've introduced a bike share program to connect our communities and updated our parks and pedestrian access as well. Through a public health grant from Health & Human Services, we partnered with Applied Wayfinding to design more than 50 two-sided wayfinding signs, and used city funds to install these throughout the downtown area—all in the spirit of making these locations vibrant, safer, and attractive for residents.

But perhaps one of the most visible symbols of Springfield's resurgence has been the $94 million restoration of Union Station, our regional intermodal transit hub, originally built in 1926. This jewel of the city reopened in 2017 after being shuttered due to neglect for more than 40 years, and it is the linchpin of our transit strategy. Serving around 100,000 rail passengers annually, it features service for several Amtrak routes such as the Northeast Corridor, Vermonter, and Lake Shore Limited. It also serves as the new hub for the Pioneer Valley Transit Authority, Peter Pan Bus Lines (which operates its headquarters here), Greyhound Lines, and the Hartford Line commuter rail.

U.S. Rep. Richard Neal deserves a great deal of credit for shepherding through legislation to deliver key portions of the funding for Union Station, and he continues to advocate for transportation equity along the Boston-Worcester-Springfield-Pittsfield corridor. An early 2020 study by the Massachusetts Department of Transportation looks at the feasibility of adding an East-West rail link and is raising some hopes throughout Western Massachusetts about the ability to provide a fast, comfortable, and reliable way to commute to and from Boston. The impact on Springfield's economy and the opportunities extended to our residents would be immense.

On the education front, residents benefit from the city's substantial commitment to physically rebuilding our schools, some of which were originally built in the 1800s. In partnership with the Massachusetts School Building Authority, Springfield secured sizeable reimbursements of $336 per square foot (based on a total cost of $500 per square foot) for each build and has overseen an investment of more than $750 million in public school infrastructure. Since 2007, we have built eight new schools from the ground up and provided substantial updates to others. New facilities include Brightwood Elementary School, Elias Brookings School, Forest Park Middle School, Lincoln Elementary School, Mary A. Dryden Veterans Memorial School, and Roger L. Putnam Vocational Technical Academy. William N. DeBerry School and Homer Street School are next to be rebuilt. While other cities are tearing schools down, we are building them up. With close to 60 schools in the district, it is pretty incredible to see 15% turning over in around 10 years.

Further, a MassMutual Foundation grant helped us extend the reach of Boston College's national City Connects program in Springfield Schools. The program provides support for students and their families by connecting them with existing community resources and support services (e.g., mental health services, mentoring, after-school activities) rather than tasking our schools with creating a new program. In 2020, City Connects counselors were placed in 28 of our public schools. As the district works to expand the offering, we are filling about five to six new positions each year.

Additionally, through an innovative public/private partnership with the federal Head Start program, Square One, and the YMCA of Greater Springfield, the city purchased a former preschool for $2.6 million to launch an full-day preschool program for 350 students—offered at no charge to families. The School Department was able to hire 22 education professionals using its own savings to bring this facility to life. More recently, we opened the $14 million Educare Springfield facility through a foundation grant to provide a state-of-the-art learning experience for children from birth to age 5. The facility will be supported by the Buffett Early

Childhood Fund and is just the 24th of its kind in the country—and the only such facility in Massachusetts.

These two facilities filled a crucial need, especially in a high-poverty city like ours, by better preparing young children for kindergarten. As we've improved across many aspects of education, our schools' graduation rates have climbed. From pre-K to 12th grade, our city and our schools have made tremendous strides, and we are now better positioned than ever to sustain and increase that momentum.

The Place to Work

Of course, like any city, the willingness of people to move to Springfield also depends on our ability to attract and retain businesses that can provide a range of jobs: education, healthcare, manufacturing, technology, services, and more. To borrow an analogy, a city's economy is like a shark: It either moves forward or it dies. Fortunately, Springfield has moved forward and performed very well.

Perhaps one of our most high profile "wins" came when CRRC, a more than $30 billion company and the world's largest supplier of rail transit equipment, decided to establish its North American hub in Springfield. The 204,000-square-foot facility, which sits on a 40-acre site in the eastern section of the city, opened in 2017 following a $95 million investment. It's exciting to us because the CRRC manufacturing facility is employing more than 200 skilled workers. These are well-paying manufacturing jobs, with an average annual salary of $65,000, and employees are equipped with new knowledge and tools to build state-of-the-art railcar vehicles for transit agencies across the country.

In fact, since 2014, CRRC MA has been awarded contracts to supply 741 railcars nationwide. The initial mandate is to manufacture 404 subway trains for the Massachusetts Bay Transportation Authority, which is the nation's first and oldest transit system. But the factory will also build 64 subway cars for the Los Angeles County Metropolitan Transit Authority (with an option for hundreds more) and 45 double-decker commuter rail vehicles for the Southeastern Pennsylvania Transportation Authority. Congressman Neal, our tireless advocate in Washington, has also been instrumental in writing legislation to help keep this facility operating after it drew criticism from opponents.

Springfield is also home to other major regional and national companies, including Baystate Health (which opened its TechSpring center in 2014 to ignite healthcare innovation in the region), Big Y Supermarkets, Liberty Mutual, Mercy Hospital, Merriam-Webster, and The Massachusetts Mutual Life Insurance Company, which is our city's second largest employer, founded in Springfield in 1851 and ranked No. 89 on the 2020 Fortune 500 list. MassMutual employs more than 7,500 people nationwide, and in early 2020 CEO Roger Crandall indicated the Springfield campus would grow from 3,500 to 4,500 employees over the coming two years, bringing even greater economic support to our city and region.

To say that MassMutual has been a longtime, stalwart supporter of Springfield is a major understatement. From purchasing the naming rights to our 8,000-seat multi-purpose arena, the MassMutual Center, to providing timely assistance during the 2011 tornado, and giving generously through its foundation, Mass-Mutual has been a pillar of our community.

One such contribution from the MassMutual Foundation helped support the $6 million Springfield Innovation Center (mentioned in Chapter 2), which opened in 2018 through a partnership between MassDevelopment and DevelopSpringfield. To further support the region's growing need for a qualified technology workforce, Springfield has committed to ensuring that skills-building and educational opportunities are available for all citizens at all levels and ages—and the Springfield Innovation Center does just this. Its primary focus is on helping prepare Springfield for civic continuity in the event of another natural disaster. Similarly, the Tech Foundry located on Main Street has trained more than 250 students since its founding in 2014, elevating underrepresented groups into sustainable careers and contributing to a growing IT ecosystem in Springfield.

Our colleges and universities also play a vital role. An educational consortium composed of the eight public and private colleges in the area make up the Cooperating Colleges of Greater Springfield, enhancing the local community through shared programs, talents, and facilities. These include American International College, Bay Path University, Elms College, Holyoke Community College, Springfield College, Springfield Technical Community College, Western New England University, and Westfield State University. Along with the UMass Center at Springfield and Cambridge College, which has a campus in Springfield, these institutions collectively make up Springfield's Knowledge Corridor.

As our community has rebounded, enrollment is on the rise. At the start of the 2017–18 academic year for instance, Springfield College announced its enrollment had grown approximately 22%, and that the incoming class of 2021 was its largest to date.

The Place to Play

Of course, Springfield is much more than a great place to live and work. We enjoy a remarkable number of ways to enrich ourselves with sports, concerts, museums, dining, theater, gaming, and more. From Springfield Symphony Hall and the Mass-Mutual Center to our five museums and downtown dining district, Springfield offers enormous resources to visitors and residents alike.

The dominant centerpiece is MGM Springfield—a $960 million, 250-room hotel and casino complex that opened in 2018. The 2 million-square-foot complex sits on a three-block site that was previously devastated by the 2011 tornado. In many ways, MGM Springfield symbolizes the turnaround our city has achieved, from adversity to advantage.

The facility contains a gaming area surrounded by a parking garage, hotel, spa, movie theater, restaurants, and shops. The 125,000-square-foot casino is home to 2,550 slots, 120 table games, and a poker room. In its first year, the casino brought 6 million visitors to Springfield, as well as headlining performers like Aerosmith and Cher. Most importantly, our host city agreement ensures that Springfield is guaranteed to receive from MGM (in lieu of property taxes or revenue sharing) about $25 million each year for 40 years—a cumulative total of nearly $960 million. This money will provide us additional opportunities to further improve the city.

Adding to the local culture, the Springfield Museums consortium operates the George Walter Vincent Smith Art Museum, the Springfield Science Museum, the Michele and Donald D'Amour Museum of Fine Arts, the Lyman and Merrie Wood Museum of Springfield History, and—perhaps our best-known stop—The Amazing World of Dr. Seuss Museum. A $7 million capital campaign brought this facility to life in 2017. It's the only museum devoted exclusively to Springfield's own native son, Theodore Geisel—a.k.a. Dr. Seuss—and offers a range of family-friendly exhibits that let visitors explore the life and works of the great children's author while experimenting with new sounds and vocabulary. It's been a smash hit. Attendance at Springfield Museums doubled from the previous year, with visitors arriving from every state in the union and 17 countries. Locals have taken notice, too: Massachusetts visitations rose 37% and Springfield residents enjoy free admission. Collectively, our five museums contribute $16 million in economic activity to the city—a figure that today is significantly higher than in years past.

Springfield is also embracing the arts in other significant ways. In fact, Springfield is one of the top 10 cities in New England for employing creative workers. The Springfield Central Cultural District is a major initiative of the Springfield Cultural Partnership that aims to foster greater support of the arts and arts education in the city by creating and sustaining a vibrant cultural environment and engaging institutions, artists, and the community. More than 500,000 people visit Springfield each year exclusively for art-related events, and we've added more than 30 new public art installations in downtown within a two-year span. In our schools, too, we've bucked the prevailing national trend and added 38 full-time employees to reinvigorate music and arts programs across our district, helping to produce more well-rounded students from elementary school on up. Ultimately, the arts and cultural institutions bring a $50 million direct economic impact to the city and support more than 1,800 jobs.

Another art-related improvement is happening on Main Street. The Paramount Theater, built in 1926, will undergo a $41 million renovation to restore this grand Classical Revival venue, which is listed on the National Register of Historic Places and has seen performances from greats like B.B. King, Billy Joel, and James Brown. Work is already underway to create a 1,750-seat performing arts center that will open in 2021. The attached Massasoit House—an 85-room hotel—will also be restored.

To complement these improvements, we set aside a $1.5 million loan fund to foster a downtown dining district and are using these funds to add more food and drink options—like sushi and ramen at BarKaya, pub fare at Naismith's, and Springfield's first craft beer brand, White Lion Brewery. These new options will supplement longtime local favorites like Theodore's and The Fort. Each applicant can receive a loan of up to $200,000 to launch their own establishment.

Further, tapping into MassDevelopment's Transformative Development Initiative (TDI), which is a program designed for "Gateway Cities" like ours to accelerate economic growth through partnerships, planning, and community engagement, we have turned our downtown into a hub of cultural and community activity. Coined the "Springfield TDI District," here we are inviting entrepreneurship, creating jobs and opportunities for small-business development, and bringing restaurants and retail storefronts to the heart of our city. In short, we've transformed downtown into a destination.

One of our signature programs in connection with the TDI partnership is Make-It Springfield, which opened in 2016 as a 30-day pop-up project in downtown that simply never shut down. Still going strong in 2020, Make-It Springfield provides a space for local makers, artists, entrepreneurs, programmers, students, and enthusiasts to make, create, and share their skills and tools. The TDI partnership has also helped to foster the creation of a nonprofit startup accelerator, Valley Venture Mentors.

Finally, like any Massachusetts community, Springfield is home to thousands of sports fans, and two sports have an incredibly strong legacy in our city: hockey and basketball.

Hockey has a rich history in the city, dating back to the 1920s when it became home to the Springfield Indians, an American Hockey League (AHL) franchise purchased and operated for more than 30 years by NHL legend Eddie Shore. Today, the AHL operates its league headquarters in Springfield, and we hosted the AHL's 2019 All-Star Classic, drawing sellout crowds and showcasing our city's elite hockey heritage. Of course, Springfield continues to enjoy its own AHL team: The Springfield Thunderbirds, which play in the MassMutual Center and attract roughly 5,000 fans per game. In fact, when our previous team, the Springfield Falcons, left in 2016, dozens of local businesses banded together to purchase the Thunderbirds so local hockey fans wouldn't miss a season.

Springfield is also famous for its basketball heritage. One of our most famous citizens, Dr. James Naismith, invented basketball on the campus of Springfield College, and the city is home to the Naismith Memorial Basketball Hall of Fame situated along the Connecticut River. It celebrates every level of men's and women's basketball in a 40,000-square-foot museum that draws more than 200,000 visitors annually. In two separate initiatives totaling $35 million, the Basketball Hall of Fame is undergoing a multi-phase refurbishment to its physical facilities and we are investing in new interactive displays and technology for fans and visitors to enjoy.

★ ★ ★

No one wants to say that Springfield has it all figured out. Challenges remain and we will continue to strive to bring stability, safety, and prosperity to every corner of the city. It's equally true, however, that we have made enviable progress. All told, Springfield hosts more than 10 million visitors every year to various attractions and facilities, which means these worthy investments that became possible only once we gained control of our budgets, processes, and expenses will continue to pay dividends to our city and citizens.

Springfield earned its highest rating in city history in 2019 from Standard & Poor's: an AA- rating with a stable outlook. S&P praised our city's very strong financial management, strict adherence to financial policies and procedures, and excellent budgetary performance. The success of our reinvigorated finances and data-driven approach to managing the city's workforce—coupled with an influx of FEMA money following the 2011 tornado—gave us new and remarkable latitude to invest in all of these projects and infrastructure improvements, putting a bright face on this turnaround that was visible to the city and the region.

CHAPTER SEVEN

The Road Forward:
Best Days Ahead for Springfield

After flipping a $41 million deficit into a $50 million surplus, upgrading our city's credit rating, recovering from a devastating tornado, and spurring more than $3 billion in economic development, the temptation to take a victory lap was, at times, strong. After all, we have achieved so much in Springfield in the face of some strong headwinds and more than a few naysayers.

But the reality is this: While I firmly believe Springfield's best days are ahead, we have a great deal of work to confront in the next 5–10 years. We have addressed many critical short-term challenges, but long-term issues remain—almost all revolving around stubborn financial situations that will require patience and perseverance. We didn't fall into these problems overnight, and we won't solve them overnight either.

The Taxation Challenge

In the decade following the Great Recession in 2008, by many measures the United States largely recovered: stock markets reached record-high levels as unemployment reached record lows, and interest rates stabilized. But Springfield struggled to fully regain its financial footing.

You see, for many municipalities, most revenue is derived from property taxes—but according to Massachusetts law (Proposition 2½), that revenue is capped at 2.5% of the assessed value of all property. Following the recession, property values in Springfield did not recover to pre-2008 levels until early 2020. In fact, from 2008 to 2010, the city lost 10.4% of the full and fair cash value of all taxable real estate and personal property, reducing our maximum tax capacity by $20 million. That trend slowed, but continued all the way until 2014. By then the loss in value had reached 14.2% and a reduced tax capacity of $27.8 million.

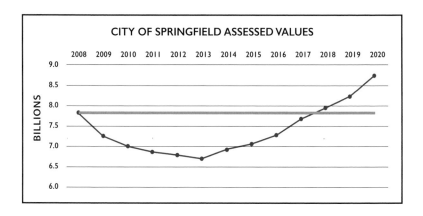

Even though we have executed a robust economic development plan for Springfield and increased taxable values, these gains have not fully translated into new revenue for the city because of Proposition 2½. After all, economic development, at least in the short term, brings an increase in municipal expenses as demand on city services spikes. Without the ability to levy new taxes on the economic growth created in Springfield, we struggle to offset the costs.

Springfield lost an estimated $26 million of new growth levy capacity over the past six years and is projected to face perpetual deficits of $10–15 million in the years to come—simply due to the way the law requires our city to calculate taxes. These losses translate into layoffs, furloughs, wage and hiring freezes, and delayed capital and infrastructure investments. The ability to add $4–5 million in new growth above the levy ceiling would go a long way in enabling us to provide core services to citizens. But as things stand, with nondiscretionary costs such as health insurance and retirement payments crowding out other budgetary needs and creating operating challenges, these types of sacrifices don't go unnoticed in an urban landscape where we struggle financially to maintain a consistent level of service.

Not willing to stand down, in 2019 the city proposed legislation that would allow access to a new growth levy capacity. We believe that if Springfield is successful in creating new economic development, the additional revenue our city generates should not count against the statutory levy limit. Gaining access to certified new growth levy capacity will help balance the cost of increasing service, while creating a friendly and exciting environment to capitalize on economic development. And the future is promising, as Gov. Baker's administration is set to review the legislation to analyze the impact Proposition 2½ has had on municipal budgets, and potentially make recommendations to mitigate those constraints.

	Previous Year Levy Limit	Amended FY 2012 Growth	Amended Levy Limit * 2.5%	Current FY New Growth	Current FY Potential Levy†	Current FY Levy Ceiling	Lost Levy
FY7	138,488,062	7,582	3,462,391	3,592,680	145,550,715	185,841,263	
FY8	145,550,715	293,119	3,646,096	4,016,102	153,506,032	195,178,563	
FY9	153,506,032	18,132	3,838,104	5,735,227	163,097,495	181,031,865	
FY10	163,097,495	57,621	4,078,878	3,590,038	170,824,032	174,870,473	
FY11	170,824,032	21,561	4,271,140	3,482,214	178,598,947	171,233,218	(7,365,729)
FY12	171,233,218	36,842	4,281,752	4,526,534	180,078,346	169,400,199	(10,678,147)
FY13	169,400,199	211,806	4,240,300	5,868,281	179,720,586	167,408,833	(12,311,753)
FY14	167,408,833	372,129	4,194,524	5,796,076	177,771,562	172,959,829	(4,811,733)
FY15	172,959,829	28,013	4,324,696	3,893,490	181,206,028	176,123,213	(5,082,815)
FY16	176,123,213	141,737	4,406,624	5,047,901	185,719,475	181,910,553	(3,808,922)
FY17	181,910,553	9,717	4,548,007	4,966,608	191,434,885	191,448,902	—
FY18	191,434,885	612,531	4,801,185	4,332,083	201,180,684	198,331,396	(2,849,288)
FY19	198,331,396	203,723	4,963,378	5,098,516	208,597,013	205,316,171	(3,280,842)
FY20	205,316,171	5,622	5,133,045	5,920,463	216,375,301	218,252,539	—

CITY OF SPRINGFIELD TAX LEVY CALCULATION

† If less than ceiling — **Total Lost Levy FY11–FY19: $50,189,228**

Education: Investments for the Future

In 2019, Massachusetts enacted a landmark piece of legislation. It was approved unanimously by the House and Senate and signed into law by Gov. Baker, and will reinvigorate Springfield's educational infrastructure in the coming decade. The Student Opportunity Act is an education funding bill that overhauls the state's formula for funding public education, with plans for a $1.5 billion infusion of incremental spending over seven years. It's the largest influx of new money since Massachusetts's original formula was devised in 1993. The legislation directs the bulk of its monies toward underfunded districts that have a stronger need to close achievement gaps for low-income students.

While the specifics will undoubtedly shift, the early indications are that Springfield could reap significant funding. An estimate published by the Department of Elementary and Secondary Education in October 2019 suggests that Springfield's foundation budget of $411.5 million in fiscal 2020 (of which the state pays $370.7 million) will increase to $655.4 million (of which the state would pay $605.4 million) by fiscal 2027. (Note: Due to COVID-19, funding for the Student Opportunity Act was put on hold.)

Once funded, however, we anticipate there will be many competing demands for us to manage, from unions seeking raises to regulators seeking spending accountability and measurable outcomes that meet important thresholds and milestones. But the ultimate aim of this funding is to help the district educate our students, address the rising costs of special education, teach English learners and low-income students, and cope with the rising costs of employee health benefits. There are also plans to continue investing in interventions like tutoring, student support, and additional staffing—the kinds of resources that support positive learning outcomes. The goals is to reach more students and keep them in school. We also hope to pursue innovation in areas like dual-credit programs with local colleges, career-path programs, pipelines to partner colleges, and more, tapping into the rich educational resources and opportunities across Springfield's Knowledge Corridor.

Separately, we are extending our efforts to ensure students succeed after graduating from high school. Under the auspices of the Springfield Promise Program, public and charter school students can earn a 'Last Dollar Scholarship.' If, for example, a student's college financial aid award doesn't fully cover their tuition costs, this scholarship helps bridge that gap. A graduating senior might receive scholarships for 85–90% of the cost of college, but even a 10–15% remaining gap can be prohibitively expensive and prevent the student from enrolling. We are committed to giving students those last dollars they need to make it to college.

We launched the Last Dollar Scholarship program with a third-party management team in 2007 and allocated an $8.7 million spend-down trust to fund the program in 2009. By 2016, we had brought the program in house, where a team of counselors, educators, administrators, financial planners, and parents collaborate

SPRINGFIELD PROMISE PROGRAM: PROGRESS REVIEW					
	FAFSA Completed	SPS FAFSA Completed	Planning Sessions	FAFSA Workshops	Last Dollar Scholarship Apps
2019	1,030	926	1,057	98	133
2018	1,014	917	1,059	53	155
2017	1,101	1,009	1,203	149**	134
2016*	923	835	No Data	No Data	No Data

*2016 serviced by uAspire, prior to the City of Springfield & Springfield Public Schools partnership
**Includes a mix of during school events to support FAFSA completion at individual schools

to help students navigate the process of applying for student aid through FAFSA, tour local colleges, apply for scholarships, and secure other financial aid that they qualify for or are entitled to. The percentage of Springfield students completing FAFSA applications has steadily increased since the program's inception, and many have received awards that generally range from $500 to $2,000.

Tackling Pension Debt

The relentless march of demographics and actuarial tables are catching up with us in the form of pensions and other post-employment benefits (OPEB). Amid the Great Recession in 2008 our pension fund lost $98 million in value, and a recent analysis unfortunately confirmed that Springfield has the worst-funded pension fund in Massachusetts. Making matters worse, an even bigger line item lurks with respect to health insurance for our retirees. Our OPEB exposure is a staggering $1.5 billion, and the state expects each city to fund that obligation at 100%.

But the city is on a path to adjust our finances and address these liabilities. Pension stabilization efforts headed by Mayor Sarno's administration, and in cooperation with Springfield City Council and the state's Public Employee Retirement Administration Commission (PERAC), include an aggressive funding schedule launched in 2016 that increased funds directed to the retirement system by $20.4 million over three years (fiscal 2018 to 2020). If undeterred, the initiative will put us on a course to be fully funded by 2034.

PENSION FUNDING SCHEDULE

Fiscal Year	Pension Increase	Schedule Cost	Total Increased Contribution
FY16	6%	47,710,109	2,700,572
FY17	6%	50,572,716	2,862,607
FY18	14%	57,652,878	7,080,178
FY19	14%	65,724,281	8,071,403
FY20	9%	71,639,466	5,915,185
FY21	9%	78,087,018	6,447,552

Planning for Rainy Days

Like other cities, Springfield benefited from record economic expansion in recent years. Heading into 2020, we had set aside $50 million in stabilization reserves (two-thirds of our $75 million target) and were resting comfortably atop a strong technology foundation that would allow us to be efficient with our money and effective in delivering core services. When the tough times returned—and we knew at some point they would—we would have systems in place to help us make difficult (but always accurate) decisions. In this way, we never lost focus on preparing for lean years ahead.

And yet, the escalating chain of events that took place beginning in March of 2020 caught us off guard. We had prepared for many "rainy day" scenarios, but a global pandemic was not one of them. A nationwide economic shutdown was, until now, unfathomable. In responses to the projected revenue shortfalls emanating not only from the federal and state governments but also municipalities, Mayor Sarno announced a hiring and spending freeze on April 15, 2020. While we continued to fund emergency and essential services and maintain core city services, we otherwise conserved funds to the greatest extent possible to avoid catastrophic cuts to the pending fiscal 2021 budget. It was the fiscally responsible thing to do.

This wasn't the first punch our city has taken (and it might not be the last). We have our experience recovering from natural and man-made disasters to lean on, and technology that allows us to track all costs related to defeating COVID-19 and to go after every dime of relief and recovery reimbursement funding. We have the tools and technology to help residents and business community weather this storm, to rebuild what has been broken, and again restore Springfield's financial health. And you can bet that preparation and planning will remain key to our fiscal strategy.

★ ★ ★

The next 10 years do not lack in challenges for Springfield, yet those of us in a position to shape the future of our city remain steadfast in our belief that we have the tools, the people, and the data to rise to the occasion.

In the last decade, we regained our footing in all key areas: financial, academic, economic, social, and lifestyle. Instead of a $41 million deficit, Springfield city government created a $50 million surplus and improved our credit rating. We recovered from one of the biggest natural disasters in New England history. We brought major economic engines to Springfield and created hordes of middle-class jobs. Our public schools are regaining their vibrancy as high school graduation rates rise and college acceptances increase. We formed new and effective contracts with first responders, making our streets and our neighborhoods safer. Driving forward market-rate housing initiatives and community engagement programs, we are drawing people back to the city.

We succeeded before, and we continue to climb. No one can predict what the future holds, but in Springfield, we are far better prepared to adapt and shape our city's future than ever before.

Images Courtesy of the City of Springfield

Overlooking Court Square, Springfield City Hall was built in 1913.

Springfield is home to the Naismith Memorial Basketball Hall of Fame, which draws more than 200,000 visitors annually. (Photo courtesy of Denis Tangney Jr from iStockphoto LP)

The Connecticut River Walk and Bikeway passes through Springfield's Riverfront Park and offers direct access to the Basketball Hall of Fame via a pedestrian bridge. (Photo courtesy of Christopher Boswell from Envato Pty Ltd)

The MassMutual Center (left) and Springfield's historic Old First Church (right) border Court Square in the heart of downtown. Redevelopment of the former Court Square Hotel building (center) began in 2020 and is a critical part of the city's revitalization efforts.

On June 1, 2011, Springfield experienced the worst natural disaster in its history when an EF-3 tornado cut across seven neighborhoods, destroying more than 500 buildings and displacing hundreds of families.

Springfield received $18 million in FEMA funds to replace a severly damaged state armory building, which has since been sold to MGM Springfield.

The fully rennovated historic armory building is now a dining and entertainment space operated by the full-service MGM Springfield casino, which opened in 2017.

The $94 million restoration of Springfield Union Station, originally built in 1926, was completed in 2017.

The 204,000-square-foot CRRC railcar manufacturing facility opened its doors in Springfield in 2017.

The Springfield Museums comprise five world-class art, history, and science museums, plus a memorial to Dr. Seuss. (Photo courtesy of Springfield Museums)

The Amazing World of Dr. Seuss Museum (pictured) and the Dr. Seuss National Memorial Sculpture Garden pay tribute to Springfield native Theodor Seuss Geisel. (Photo courtesy of Springfield Museums)

In 2018, Springfield and its neighboring communities launched a regional bike share program consisting of 50 bike share stations across the Pioneer Valley.

The Fresh Paint Springfield program first added nine community-inspired murals across the city's downtown in 2019, and the program continues today.

The Springfield Culinary and Nutrition Center opened in 2019 and is operated by the school district's food service partner, Sodexo. (Photo courtesy of edm from edm-ae.com)

The Springfield Culinary and Nutrition Center prepares fresh meals for more than 30,000 city students every day. (Photo courtesy of edm from edm-ae.com)

The Roger L. Putnam Vocational Technical Academy is among eight new schools built from the ground up in Springfield since 2007. The new facility opened its doors in 2012.

Springfield Technical Community College is located on the Springfield Armory National Historic Site, home of the first American armory established in 1794. It is the only technical community college in Massachusetts and was founded in 1967.

ACKNOWLEDGMENTS

Springfield's storied history is rooted in hard work and innovation. It's our accomplishments—not the hard times—that define us. We celebrate a rich heritage, not just as the birthplace of basketball or the first 'Springfield' in the United States. Our "City of Firsts" has been the backdrop for dozens of historic inventions, new ventures, and cultural milestones. While everything my colleagues and I accomplished together may appear extraordinary—ironically, it's nothing out of the ordinary for Springfield.

To Pat Roach, my closest ally and good friend, who has stuck by my side for 14 long years as we uncovered the unimaginable and fixed the unfixable: You and I lived these pages together. You fought the battles that needed fighting; forged the public/private partnerships that have advanced our city and our schools in countless ways; embraced residents and families and created a community within our schools; and demonstrated unrelenting commitment to student welfare and success. This book, as with many other achievements, would not have been possible without you.

In addition to congratulating the Mayor on his 2019 reelection, which occurred during the time I was writing this book, and which led me to reflect on how fortunate Springfield is to have a strong leader; a leader who has trust in the people around him; who is accountable and compassionate—I send my sincerest thanks.

Partnering with UKG to pen this book, to relive old memories and recount the victories my colleagues and I have shared, has been enjoyable. Technology is not a footnote in our story. It's a linchpin—one that enabled Springfield to hold our workforce accountable to play by the rules, weed out inefficient practices, and generate millions of dollars to reinvest in our communities.

Also, a note of thanks to others who generously shared their perspective and stories: Police Commissioner Cheryl C. Clapprood; Superintendent Daniel J. Warwick; Chief Development Officer Timothy Sheehan; City Solicitor Ed Pikula; Chief of Staff Tom Ashe; Joao Alves, a teacher and administrator in our public schools; and Mike Grey and Marc Roy with our food service partner Sodexo.

ABOUT THE AUTHOR

Timothy J. Plante (TJ) is the chief administrative and financial officer (CAFO) for the City of Springfield, Massachusetts, where he directly oversees the city's financial functions and serves as the principal city management advisor to the Mayor. In 14 years of service to the city, he and his cohorts have overcome tremendous fiscal challenges, putting Springfield on the map for strong financial management.

TJ's position is one that's quite unique to Springfield. Created by state statute to ensure that progress made under the Springfield Finance Control Board between 2004 and 2009 would be maintained, the CAFO position provides complete oversight of city finances and has the power to establish efficiencies that will continue to move the city forward. Appointed to the role in 2012, TJ has called it "a perfect culmination of all my experience in both state and municipal government, which allows me to continue the work of helping run a community with assorted challenges and great possibility."

Previously, TJ served as the city's budget director, acting chief financial officer, and simultaneously held positions as the city's finance director and chief financial officer for Springfield Public Schools. Under his sustained leadership, Springfield's bond rating surged and its finance division has been consistently recognized by the Government Finance Officers Association (GFOA), receiving the Distinguished Budget Presentation Award for a 12th consecutive year in April 2020.

Prior to beginning his tenure in Springfield, TJ served the Commonwealth of Massachusetts as the state's deputy budget director for the Public Health Department, legislative director to Senate Majority Leader Frederick Berry, and as a fiscal policy analyst for the Senate Committee on Ways and Means. TJ holds a master's degree in public administration from the Sawyer School of Management at Suffolk University in Boston, Massachusetts and a bachelor's degree in political science and criminal justice from Stonehill College in Easton, Massachusetts.

TJ happily resides in Springfield with his wife Katie and their three children, Trevor, Alyssa, and Kaitlyn.